Hira Erzolia

A Wales-Cameroon Anthology

Edited by

Eric Ngalle Charles

Hafan Books

Published in 2018 by
Hafan Books
c/o Tom Cheesman
Keir Hardie Building
Swansea University
Swansea SA2 8PP   Wales   UK

www.lulu.com/hafan
t.cheesman@swansea.ac.uk

ISBN 9780995496668

Acknowledgments:

Douglas Achingale's poems are from his collection *Oppression* published in 2013 by Nyaa Publishers in Cameroon. THE HONOURABLE MINISTER won a prize in the National Book Development Council Poetry Competition in 1994.

Menna Elfyn's poems first appeared in *Perfect Blemish/Perffaith Nam, New &c Selected poems 1995-2007*, Bloodaxe Books (2007); SWALLOWS: in *Between a Mountain and a Sea* (Swansea: Hafan Books, 2003).

Humberto Gatica, EXILE (in the Introduction) from *Between a Mountain and a Sea* (Swansea: Hafan Books, 2003), and his collection *El Jardin de Arena / The Sand Garden* (Hafan Books 2008).

Des Mannay's THEY CALL ME won a Gold in the Creative Futures Literary Awards 2015; published in the anthology *Impossible Things* (2017).

Bethany Rivers: POSTED ON THE QUIET, from: *i am not a silent poet* (2017); AT SEVENTEEN published by Silver Birch Press (2017); TIME IS SOFTER published by Cinnamon Press (2012).

Gareth Writer-Davies: BREATHE from *Bodies* (Indigo Dreams, PELARGONIUM from *The Lover's Pinch* (Arenig Press, 2018); JAWCH previously published in the *London Progressive Journal* (2017).

Printed by Lulu.com

All proceeds to Swansea Asylum Seekers Support, UK charity #1175186

Contents

At every dawn,
Young voices shout against dictatorship.

At every dawn,
the gatekeeper's sword
falls on their young necks.

Why then my lord did you give us a voice?

– ENC

Eric Ngalle Charles

Introduction

How I wish to be an Ezruli
To suck nectar from hibiscus flowers
That morning breezes may blow me,
Hither and thither,
From the streams of Namonge
Behind my mother's house,
To the roof of Mongo Mo Ndemi, the giant.

I wish.

This anthology forms part of my Migration, Memory and Trauma project: a 'Bridge-Building', a creative link between Wales and Cameroon: a collection of writings by some of my favourite writers from two countries – Cameroon, where I come from, and Wales, where I've lived for most of my life.

My first poem, many years ago, was a dedication to my mother, so I thought: 'Dearest mother, / you are beautiful / like the snowflakes of Siberia, / everyone knows where you are, / no one dares' – after she read this poem, she kicked me out of her house. I lived with my maternal grandfather for two months. My mother thought I was making a mockery of the fact that many men came and left her bed chamber. Maybe I was.

I became a writer in Wales. Only recently I went back to Cameroon after seventeen years of rehabilitation here in Wales. I went to Cameroon as a writer with the help of Wales Arts International. Until then I had hardly read Cameroonian writers or met any.

7

The Welsh writers in this book helped to make me what I am, as a writer and as a person. My relationship with them is very emotional. With the Cameroonian writers it's also emotional, but in a different way.

The great poet from Iraq, Abdul Wahab Al-Bayati, said: 'love is not temporary, nor proprietary' – love exists everywhere and always, and love is beyond ownership, above all, love is an ever-present possibility. If one thing has made living in Wales all these years bearable, it is love, a love that fuelled my will to resist, to resist the temptation of suicide, an emotion that haunted me for a long time after arriving in Wales from Russia.

The first time I met a writer in Cameroon, I was in upper sixth in the Government Bilingual Grammar School in Molyko, Buea, preparing for my Advance Level Certificate examination. The whole class anticipated the coming of the late, great Mr Bate Bisong (1954-2007). When Mr Bate walked into our class, you could hear the silence. He sat in our class for two whole hours, in silence, peering at us, one by one, our hearts stopped, almost. As the bell rang, as the lesson period ended, just before he left, Mr Bate focused his attention on one girl sitting at the front of the class, he said: 'When I look at you, I think of a fish'. As brilliant a writer as Mr Bate was, his legacy looms large, he almost scared literary creativity out of us. We thought no one could be as good as him no matter how much we tried. Such elitism is still commonplace in the Cameroonian literati. When Bate Bisong spoke English, you needed an Oxford dictionary. Rest in peace, sage.

As you read through this anthology you will see that Cameroonian writers had different experiences when it came to the late 'BB', Bate Bisong: you will enjoy Kange Ernest's and Dibussi Tande's tributes to him; Douglas Achingale gives him the nickname 'Obassinjom' (a Juju imported from the Bakossi clan). My own tribute ('Hyperbole') appeared in *Poetry Wales* (Winter 2016):

I always wanted to write,
When I met Bate Besong RIP,
in upper sixth Lycée,
he said 'Ngalle, Jump'

I jumped so highhhhhhh,
didn't come down for days.
When I came down a week later,
I was Blacker than a 'Hausa butcher's toenails'

This book is a collection of writings by people I met, strangers who helped and held my hands. It's a personal journey of self-discovery, finding my name and my place in the grand scheme of things. The anthology brings together my Welsh heroes and heroines with those who are trying to have their voices heard in Cameroon, the country of my birth.

It feels great to be able to link arms between writers of the two countries I have grown to love for different reasons. It is good to extend that cross-border handshake at a time when the world is full of tension and anxiety, when patriotism is entering a nationalistic phase. I have spent half of my time on this earth as a stranger in another country, and I have felt welcomed. Today I am celebrated as a poet, a writer and playwright. My contribution to Welsh literature was finally recognised when I was awarded with the prestigious Creative Wales Award by the Arts Council of Wales. But the journey to be here in Wales was far from straightforward, in fact, it was full of turbulence: migration, memory, and trauma turbulences.

Many people have asked why I feel the need to create a literary link between Wales and Buea; between Small Soppo Wovilla, the grounds where my mother's placenta is buried, the ground that holds half of my umbilical cord and Wales, the nation, Cardiff the place that gave me a platform, a voice, the place I have a 'hiraeth' for every time I cross the Severn Bridge, every time I stay outside for more than two days.

Like my friend and mentor Jon Gower says, 'I write because I must: books might bide their time, stalk you for a few years, but eventually they will hunt you down, demanding to be written'. Thus, I have never written a poem about Buea, not really, and I do not think I have written about Small Soppo, my place of birth. The idea of this project has finally hunted me down, to demand that I put this anthology together.

I have been asked often where I got the resilience to maintain decorum, cool headedness, despite all that happened, all the various stones and sticks that life has thrown at me, how have I coped, how have I managed to come out with a smile? It is simple, as I grew up in the village of Small Soppo on the foot of Mount Cameroon, all my memory till the age of seventeen was one of love, I was loved. Love makes exile bearable and tolerable. Humberto Gartica (based in Abertawe) says in his poem 'Exile':

I abandoned
my bones
in the uncertainty
of the airports
I get lost in cities
under the nightmares of lugubrious hotels
Some night
somebody dies
in my dreams
in others
I chase my way back
to the music
of my rains
and my broken landscape.

I remember all those years ago, when my friend Greg Lewis and I sat at the offices of *South Wales Echo* as I drafted an open letter to the people of Wales, talking of how colonial winds had brought Britain to my shores. I hadn't made the distinction between Wales and the UK, I didn't know Wales had its own identity, I did not know that Wales was England's first colony (for those interested in further research, look into the Act of Union 1707).

Later I came across a speech by Adam Price, then MP for Dinefwr and East Carmarthenshire; here is an extract:

Before the Act of Union we were a conquered nation that was never fully subdued. Post-devolution we're a post-colonial country still waiting to be decolonized. It is these contradictions that describe our present predicament: we are a hybrid state living in the cracks between a dependent past and an independent future. (…) English imperialism began here in Wales; (…) the deepest legacy it has left is psychological. And (…) national liberation, if it is to mean anything, has to be a liberation of the mind. Otherwise we will be condemning ourselves to be not just the first but also the final colony.

I was very interested in Adam Price's use of the term 'hybrid state', for Cameroon is one such state, having been first visited by the Portuguese (Rios Dos Cameroes), then colonised by the Germans (Kamerun) then the English (Cameroon) and the French (Cameroun). I didn't know about Wales's colonial past. I do now.

This collection of writings brings together cultures and traditions, beyond borders and barriers, to tell the people of Wales, those that embraced me, those that fostered me, about where I came from and at the same time to tell the people of my own country about Wales. The many good deeds, the varied kindness I have received in Wales has propelled me to where I am today.

Cockroaches, worms and the underbelly of life would have eaten me whole, without Wales. I am not Black British or Black Welsh, I am a Cameroonian from the foothills of Mount Fako, but the mysteries of life now mean I can never engage in a conversation about my belonging, my roots, without mentioning Wales. Wales gave my life back, from the treacherous terrains of Russia, from the decapitation that patriarchy dealt me, Wales gave me back my voice, Wales gave me back my name and thanks to Wales, my mother no longer cries at night.

My first Welsh poem, published in the first Hafan Books publication, *Between a Mountain and a Sea* in 2003:

A Mountain and a Sea

A story from a distance.
They were my only witness,
A mountain and a sea
whose lips engulfed the green sky,
A lasting kiss,
Washing her waves offshore,
Leaving behind a boat.

That for my home-coming.

The mountain
like a giant slate,
With trees keeping vigil
Like Yomadene,
The guardian,
The mountain,
Where my grandmother
Lived after her death.
A mountain of broken hearts.

That for my home-coming.

A shinning mountain
Where sheep grazed,
By which means
My heart rejoiced.

That for my home-coming.

On a wet journey to Llandudno
Washing away pain and longing,
A re-born voice crying

Between a mountain and a sea.

Where voices echoed
Across the town's horizon
and conversation on common things.
Wake me from my slumber
then this poem
Will be over.

That for my home-coming,
Between a mountain and a sea.

This poem was inspired by the hills, the sights, sounds, the mountains, the quietude of the countryside as Tom Cheesman and I navigated some of the most beautiful landscape I have seen, from Abertawe/Swansea to Llandudno, to attend a conference organised by Academi (now called Literature Wales).

The topic of the conference was 'Literature and Trauma'. It was (as Abdallah Bashir-Khairi might have said) 'as if a mysterious courier had conveyed to the people of Wales what was taking place in my internal courts of justice'. When it was my time to speak, I was frightened, I felt lonely, but with the encouragement of Sally Baker (founder of Wales PEN Cymru) and Peter Finch I got on stage and told the audience a little about my sojourn in Russia and the cesspit of crime that was Pechatniki, Moscow. I could not bring myself then to speak of what my father's family had done to me when I was in Cameroon. At this time, I still carried that venom, that bile, I still dreamt of going back to Buea and unleashing the pogrom which I had perfected during my time in Russia, and even more so now that I could breathe in Wales and I was no longer running.

At that conference in Llandudno I first heard of Germaine Greer and the mystique that surrounded her. Fifteen years later, in the Writers Room at the Hay Festival 2017, I pointed her out to my daughter.

In Llandudno I listened to amazing speakers from around the world. A powerful poetess from Nigeria. The great Benjamin Zephaniah (I missed his reading). Renowned BBC journalist Kate Adie, just back from stints in Afghanistan and Iraq, spoke about 'Traumas of War', the ruthlessness of the Taliban, the rise of the Kurdish Peshmerga. Here in Llandudno I first heard the phrase 'Post Traumatic Stress Disorder'. At this time I did not realise I was suffering from depression or how severe it was. The word 'depressed' was not part of my vocabulary, I had never used it. The ideas of migration, memory and trauma were deep in the abyss of my heart.

A Kurdish Iranian poet spoke about the ayatollahs, the mullahs and freedom of expression. He talked about how creative writing helped him overcome his trauma. He told us the story of a beautiful donkey, his first pet, how one day he went to fetch water in a well with the donkey, he was spotted by a guard who worked for one of the mullahs, his donkey was placed on the back of an American Ford and disappeared into the desert sands. I was confused, why did this guy hate both the Americans and the mullahs?

I also listened to Farzana from Kabul. She spoke about how she and her parents had left Kabul for Uzbekistan, while in Uzbekistan their father died of a heart attack and was buried on the side of the road, her mother was raped by human traffickers several times as they could not afford to pay the traffickers. When she eventually arrived in Turkey, she was helped by a group called PEN International, who are very active in Turkey. Farzana spends her days on the south end of the Bosporus in Istanbul singing to her beloved mother who lost her sight during the migration (I think Farzana's mother lost her sight deliberately, she did not want to see the rapists as they took turns ejaculating all over her. When I was writing the play 'The Rituals of the Molikilikili' – stick insect – I thought about Farzana's mother and that nagging question: Can blindness be desired? What have those blind eyes seen to desire to see no more?) and writing beautiful poetry about the mountains of Afghanistan, and the barefoot children of Kabul. At one point as she spoke of her ordeal, Farzana cried, my goodness, we all had our handkerchiefs out. Farzana's was the last event of the evening, Tom rushed outside of the amphitheatre and he lit a cigarette. This was my first experience of the manifestation of trauma.

The article I wrote in the *South Wales Echo* all those years ago and the poem 'Between a Mountain and a Sea' became the first knot I tied in my attempt to link Wales my new home and the place of my birth. In my mind, as Chinua Achebe says, I had gathered firewood; I needed a rope to tie it and carry it home for my mother to make fire, and here in Wales the perfect rope was handed to me. There was once a time when I had gathered firewood and the only rope that was offered me was the Black Mamba. It took travelling from

Abertawe to Llandudno for me to start remembering the noises, the sights, the sounds, that planted the creative seeds in my mind all those years ago, as I crawled around the dusty floors of my mother's living room, as I watched in awe as the wall gecko waited patiently for the moth to settle before eating it. The sight of sheep grazing: 'How my heart rejoiced.' I had a goat, I loved that goat, I named it 'Evenya Mboli'; it was killed by a very greedy village hunter …

In my village of Small Soppo itself, unlike the estate in Ely where I lived, there are no traffic lights, no zebra crossings (I saw traffic lights and zebra crossings in Yaoundé, the capital of Cameroon, no one respects them, during my visit in August last year I almost got ran over by a taxi as I leisurely crossed a zebra crossing in Yaoundé), there are neither street signs nor street names, in my village, almost all the men are dead. Lack of medical diagnosis means the cause of death is left in the hands of the Juju man, whose verdict is always the same: the cause of death is witchcraft. Families will then spend monies moving from one witch doctor to another searching for the killer or killers. Please, do not laugh, this is not funny, we grew up like this, our childhood was one of terror, we were told that those who died because of witchcraft roamed the village at nights looking for those who killed them. Can you imagine?

I only learned the word 'single parent' when I moved to Cardiff. We have no names for 'single parents', for most of us 'our mothers are our fathers'. Most women after giving birth lose their names, they simply become

Ngalle's mother, Efeti's or Njoffi's mother, or they become 'mami puff' or 'mami tomatoes' depending on what she traded in the market to make ends meet. Peter Moki's mother is known simply as 'Mami Mbanga' because she sold palm nuts in the markets. If someone is looking for my mother for example, the conversation will go something like this: 'I am looking for that woman who gave birth to that stubborn child, with the big belly, you know that boy who always cries, he looks a bit like he's got witchcraft?' 'O, you mean Mama Ngalle?' 'Yes, Mama Ngalle.' 'Okay, just carry on walking down this road, go down the hill, you will come across a brown dog resting under an abandoned military truck, keep walking past the bridge, the first house on the left belongs to Mami Mbanga, once you go past Mami Mbanga, you will come across a cow that has one missing eye, the next house belongs to Mama Ngalle.' By the time you get all this, you might as well just give up.

I was going to say, if you were carrying a letter, you might as well just put the letter into the bins, then I realised we do not have public bins. We have one long road that meanders, and no one knows where it starts nor where it ends, we have no heroes, heroines are non-existent, we have no parks were children congregate to play, actually no, we had one park, we named it 'Ajax Maija ma Ngowa's stadium', Ajax's pigs blood stadium, I am not sure why that name, but it was. It was our meeting place every Sunday, we played football and enjoyed local gossips, it. was whilst playing here one Sunday that I first saw Beatrice

(Beatrice and I became very good friends). Now I hear that piece of land has been sold by the chief, it now has houses and a narrow lane that takes you up to Borstal institute for young offenders.

It was also whilst playing on that land that I first heard the name Cardiff. My distant uncle obtained a scholarship in 1986 to study maths at Cardiff University, he came back to the village and joined us to play football, and during the break he told us about watching the 1990 World Cup quarter finals between Cameroon and England in Cardiff University. Mr Gobina Elive Francis is now a maths teacher at Fitzalan High School in Cardiff.

When I first moved to Ely in Cardiff a few months after arriving in Wales, my wife would say to me, 'Eric, did you take Nicole to the park today?' Hahaha, it did not occur to me that I had to take Nicole to the park, my wife goes into a fit of rage, shouting 'Eric, why are you always neglecting your duties? In this country, men take children to the park.' I learned my lesson, I took Nicole to the park and when Jolie was born, I took her to the park. I loved going to the park, I escaped from my wife.

With this anthology, I hope to bring Cameroonian writing to Wales and beyond. This anthology is trying to say 'Diolch yn fawr iawn' and 'Tengi zraizrai' to my Welsh friends and family and take them on a journey of migration and memory, back to that tree, that tall Jack Fruit tree that imposes its shadow on my mother's kitchen. The tree is no longer there, and my mother's kitchen seemed to have shrunken.

This is not an attempt to create a literary link between Africa and Wales. This has been done. My friend and mentor **Jon Gower** went on an African safari to make a film about 'the Great Snake Migration'. Once the snakes started coming out of their holes, frightened Mr Gower dropped his camera in a snake hole in Tanzania. When I told Jon about my encounter with the Rhinoceros viper in my village when I was out hunting with my dog, he had nightmares for days. Mr Gower makes me laugh.

This anthology brings a small part of Cameroonian creativity to Wales and vice versa, to say thank you to both for propelling me into the world. The title combines 'Hiraeth' in Welsh and 'Erzolirzoli' in Bakweri, my mother tongue. (Ezruli is a bird, the smallest member of the sunbird family.) 'Hiraeth' is a central theme in Welsh poetry and song, a feeling of something lost, missing, identity or language. Wherever I find myself, I have that longing, that *hiraeth*, double: one for where I was born, and one for Wales, the land that provided me with a canopy, a bed, a pillow upon which to rest and purge my system and start again.

The poem 'Hiraeth' by **Bethany Rivers**, in this anthology, really brings home the deeper meaning of the Welsh word and the similar idea in Bakweri. *Erzolirzoli*, like hiraeth and the Portuguese *saudade*, describes a deep emotional state of nostalgic or profound melancholic longing for an absent something or someone that one loves. Erzolirzoli is an integral part of exile, when someone dies, those left behind suffer extreme erzolirzoli as it carries a repressed knowledge that the object of longing will never return. When I was gone for as long as I did, my mother and sibling had erzolirzoli for me and I for them, that constant longing kept alive by love.

I met Bethany Rivers in Cardiff, my goodness I enjoyed her reading her work, how softly spoken she was. She is a creative writing tutor and a poetry therapy practitioner. She is one of those who paved the way for me in Wales.

I first met **Mike Jenkins** during an event organised by Cardiff Central library, he read from his latest publication, I enjoyed his work. A couple of weeks later Mike invited me to perform in a pub in Merthyr where they have a monthly open mic – what a night, up until then I had never been to Merthyr. I am very happy Mike is contributing to this anthology, in three of his languages – Welsh, English, and Valleys English. I think it was also in Merthyr I met the prize-winning poet and gardener **Gareth Writer-Davies**.

I have met many people in Wales who have guided and are still guiding me, who believed and still believe in me, the truth is I wouldn't have, I couldn't have come this far without their support. I have received more help from strangers I met along the way than I have had from my family, both sides. My mother and some of her children prayed for me, whilst some wished death upon me. (I know you.) My father's family wished me dead, some wanted me extinct; but some under the ancestral shrine begged the gods to keep me safe.

I first met with **Grahame Davies** the Welsh Bard at the BBC studios in Llandaff. I was not greeted as a stranger, he shook my hands tight, then he hugged me, he took me into the BBC café and said I could have anything I wanted. I looked around, I did not recognise anything that was on offer, I asked for coffee, not the kind of coffee I tasted at Heathrow airport when I arrived in July 1999, I asked for white coffee and two sugars with lemon cake. Grahame showed me around the BBC studios; during this tour I first met Selma Chalabi who helped and recorded some of our poetry performances in Riverside, Cardiff. Grahame took me across the road to BBC Cymru; he was department head at the time. The last time I met him was in his house, I asked if one day he will be given the title National Poet of Wales, he laughs. I don't think some parts of the Welsh literati are happy with the fact that Grahame now works for the Prince of Wales.

At the BBC studios in Llandaff Grahame introduced me to Heledd's Song and the poem 'Afflicted, Abercuawg', from the Four Ancient Books of Wales. When I visited Tom Cheesmen in Swansea to discuss our first book project (*Between a Mountain and a Sea*), guess what happened, Tom brought the poem 'Afflicted, Abercuawg'. I was taken aback by the lamentation of a Welsh sage in the 8th or 9th century. Some lines in the poem have stuck with me forever:

My spirit craves to sit a long time on a hill
Not that I will up and go:
My journey now is short, my home desolate.

Piercing the winds in this barren place.

The woods dress in summer's fair colours.
I lie feverish today. (…)

Noisy the birds, damp the valleys,
Long the night. What's rare is praised;
And I deserve the reward of age: sleep. (…)

This poem reminded me of the dreams I use to have as a child. In the morning as, one opens the front door of the living room in my mother's house, the first thing that greets one's eyes is the giant which is Mount Cameroon, or as it is known amongst my clan, the Bakweri people, Mount Fako. Mount Fako is the thirty-first most prominent peak in the world, also known as Mongo Mo Ndemi: Mountain of Greatness.

When the Portuguese boats first caressed the shores of Cameroon, the first thing they saw was Mount Fako. Shocked by the sudden appearance of strangers on her shores, Mount Fako spewed fire; she erupted, shouting 'Pergunte os barcos Portuguese!'

Yes,
When they kissed her shores,
Mount Fako burst in flames,
Shouting,
Where are my daughters?
Where are my sons?

A bleached Agama lizard swallowed her womb.

The River Mungo will cry
Thick coagulated blood,
Red in rage,
Ask the Portuguese Ships.

The Portuguese, having never experienced a volcanic

23

eruption before, christened Mount Fako 'the Chariot of Gods', their curiosity took them up the mountain towards the Savannah, the villagers had deserted their villages and headed towards the flat lands. All but one Portuguese were swallowed by fierce magma and lava.

On a clear day, you can see trees on the Savannah. Growing up we were told the trees formed a fence that protected Yomadene, a god. (During the winter of 1998 in Pechatniki, Moscow, I was christened Yomadene by Johnson Likambi.) We were also told whilst growing up that at the highest point of the mountain, gods congregated in the rainy season to decide the fate of humankind, maybe this was what the Portuguese had experienced.

As we drove across Wales on our way back from Llandudno, I was home, the mountains that appeared and disappeared like mirages, 'how my spirit craved to sit on top of a hill', I was tired, the burden of my two years two months in Russia was taking its toll, I fell asleep, I dreamt, in my dream I saw my grandmother rearranging flowers on my grave, she was re-writing the words on my epitaph, 'Ngalle was here, now no more', I saw girls, I saw boys dancing bare feet in the rain, I saw women washing clothes in the small stream that runs from the mountain all the way to Limbe (colonial name Victoria) via Tole, I saw bees pregnant with nectar, carrying me home away from exile. When I woke up, we were in Abertawe.

This anthology celebrates that which connects us as humans regardless of the socio-political goings-on. Cameroon today is on the brink, the colonial divide between France and England is threatening the nation. As we speak, people have been locked up indiscriminately, many people shot and killed, most of them young and disillusioned, people jumping out of bushes killing soldiers, soldiers retaliating, 'Facebook Warriors' fanning the flames of the divide from their safe hideouts in the diaspora. For almost two years now children have paid the price of this colonial fight, they have not been allowed to go to school; in fact, schools have been burnt down. I march with Cardiff People's Assembly against austerity, against government cuts, I cannot march or even ask for school resumption in Cameroon, those who advocate for school resumption have themselves been targeted. As Chinua Achebe said: 'When two elephants fight, it is the grass that suffers.' The grass is dying in Cameroon.

When I read a good poem, I feel revived, energised, a good story takes my mind to places I dare visit only in dreams. I am hoping within this anthology, you follow each writer, each contributor as they weave magic with words, as we criss-cross continents with Grahame Davies as a 'Rough Guide', or Menna Elfyn with 'Swallows', or we weave through the dreams of a child in Isabel Adonis's 'Sweet Shop', or we see Cameroon's political system that feeds on its own inefficiencies, through the critical lenses of Douglas Achingale, or see street boys in Kampala through the eyes of Ifor ap Glyn, the National Poet of Wales since 2016.

Ifor ap Glyn is a celebrated television presenter and Welsh-language poet, bilingual in Welsh and English. He was Children's Poet Laureate for Wales in 2008-

2009 and won the Crown at the National Eisteddfod of Wales in 1999 and 2013. I love Ifor's poetry, particularly 'Harvest 1917'. After the Cricieth Festival of Words, Ifor told me about the soldier poet Hedd Wyn, and the owners of Palas Print bookshop in Caernarfon took us to visit Hedd Wyn's place of birth in the village of Trawsfynnwdd, where we met his last surviving relative, eerie.

The universal thread that ties all the writers in this anthology is their love for creative writing. I met Dr **Adeola Dewis** when I was part of a creative workshop in Grange Town Hub with Andrea Heath's Small Libraries Project, supported by South Riverside Development Centre, When I read Adeola's writings, my heart dances, I think of migratory foot prints, the memories of ancient sounds, ancient mystics, lost and found. She is a Trinidadian artist based in Cardiff. Her work looks at Trinidad Carnival performance and the translation of its self-empowering effects for art making and art presentation within the UK.

Douglas Achingale (aka Lord Havoc) has been nicknamed a 'protest poet' because of his lamentations on the current political crises in Cameroon, in fact when I ran my first creative writing workshop in Cameroon, I was shocked but not surprised that most of the writings that came out of the workshops were a scathing attack on the socio-political climate of the country. Prior to meeting Douglas in Yaoundé, I had been introduced to the great man via social media by my very good friend Dr Tonge Ebai. I was looking forward to meeting the Mr Achingale when I visited

Cameroon in August 2017. We met at a small restaurant in the Obili neighbourhood in Yaoundé where he treated me to what we call *khati-khati*, a dish of vegetables, pounded maize meal and chicken; to help with the digestion, he also bought me a bottle of Guinness. We spoke about Cameroon and its current literary climate. He signed copies of his books *Before I Die* (a poetry collection) and *A Wrong Decision* (a satirical play about Cameroon's institutions of higher learning: 'one a playground for thieves and pickpockets, the other for teachers'). Jon Gower is currently in the process of translating *Before I Die* into the Welsh language. In his poems, Mr Achingale warns the greedy before the hangman comes. When I read his poems, I think of Babatunde the soothsayer in Ola Rotimi's *The Gods Are Not to Blame* – for truly, Mr Achingale is a soothsayer.

Isabel Adonis and I have not met despite corresponding since 2003 when she contributed to our very first anthology, *Between a Mountain and a Sea*. She is an artist, writer and educator, has published in *New Welsh Review*, *Urban Welsh* (Parthian 2005), *Journal of Caribbean Literatures* (2009) among others, and her memoir *And... a conjunction of history and imagination* came out in 2010.

Nsah Mala is the author of four poetry collections: *Chaining Freedom* (2012), *Bites of Insanity* (2015), *If You Must Fall Bush* (2016), and *Constimocrazy: Malafricanising Democracy* (2017). In 2016, his story 'Christmas Disappointment' won a prize from the Cameroonian Ministry of Arts and Culture. In 2017, his poem, 'Servants de l'état' won the Malraux Prize in France. He was invited to the Caine Prize Workshop in Rwanda in 2018. Writing in English and French, he has been widely published in Cameroon, Nigeria, France, USA, Canada, and India. His poetry collection in French is forthcoming.

I met **Zillah Bowes** first at the Hay Festival in May 2017 and again when I was invited to see her perform as a featured poet in Roath, Cardiff. Zillah is a writer and filmmaker. Her poems have been published in magazines and anthologies including *Mslexia*, *The Next Review* and *Tate Modern*. She received a New Writer's Award from Literature Wales in 2014 and a Creative Wales Award from the Arts Council of Wales in 2017. She was selected for the Writers at Work programme at Hay Festival in 2016/17.

Dibussi Tande is a prolific Cameroonian writer and poet whose poems have appeared in numerous anthologies. He is the author of *No Turning Back: Poems of Freedom 1990-1993* and co-editor of *Their Champagne Party Will End! Poems in Honor of Bate Besong*.

I met sage **Menna Elfyn** in 2003 during the launch of our first anthology, which included 'Swallows' – written in Welsh and translated by her into English, a very unusual thing for her to do. I met Menna again in Caernarfon during the Gwyl Arall festival in 2016 and during the Wales PEN Cymru event at the Hay Festival in 2017. For all her greatness, her giant status, Menna is gentle. I love Menna Elfyn. She is a Welsh poet, playwright, columnist, and editor. Elfyn has published ten volumes of poetry and a dozen more of children's books and anthologies. She has also written eight plays for the stage, six radio plays for the BBC, and two plays and several documentaries for television. It was an honour to take part in the BBC Radio 4 programme with Menna, 'Hiraeth' in 2017.

Sally Baker (my Welsh Mother) of Wales PEN Cymru arranged for me to perform at the Gwyl Arral Festival in Caernarfon, paired with Ifor ap Glyn, the National Poet of Wales. I first thought Sally's email must be spam. I met the great man at Palas Print bookshop café, he shook my hands, offered me a cup of coffee, signed me a copy of his first attempt at prose, *Tra Bo Dau* (When We Were Two). In one of the most famous pubs in Caernarfon, The Black Boy, he bought me a pint of Guinness, rump steak and chips, I was in awe, here I was with the National Poet of Wales, just a normal human being. In Cameroon a person with such title will be treated like a demi-god. In The Black Boy, Ifor told me the story of a rabbit that abandoned its clan, only to come back years later speaking in a foreign accent. I adapted this story as my contribution to the 'Brexit' anthology to be published by Parthian Books. It was from Ifor that I first learned the phrase 'using Sellotape to fix broken biscuits'.

Jon Gower introduced me to **Dylan Moore**, a poet and writer who works across schools in Wales raising awareness of the plight of refugees, also an English teacher, editor at the Institute for Welsh Affairs, and he was recently named the Hay Festival International Fellow 2018-2019. When we met at the Hay Festival in 2016, the conversation went like this:

– Hello Eric, nice to meet you at last.

– Mr Moore, lovely meeting you too.

– I hear you are from Cameroon.

– Yes, I am.

– Which part of Cameroon are you from?

– I'm from the South West Province.

– No way! Where exactly from the South West?

– I'm from Buea.

– Nooo wayyy!! Where exactly in Buea?

– Longstreet Small Soppo.

– Noooooo wayyyyyyy!!!!

(I was starting to get worried as to where the conversation was going. Was he one of those people who start telling me how they had been to 'Africa' to go and help 'the poor people of Africa' and how 'Africa has so much to give'…? One of the most difficult conversations I have had was in Swansea after an event at Volcano Theatre. I was drinking a Guinness at the bar when this elderly gentleman approached me, told me how he had criss-crossed the African continent with the British Army and how he had killed Africans in Kenya during the Mau Mau uprising, and had helped quell rebellions in Sierra Leone and Liberia. Then the punchline: 'So Mr Charles, tell me, have you ever killed a person?')

Dylan continued: 'Eric, you won't believe me when I tell you this, I proposed to my wife when we were out there in Cameroon, in Buea, and Longstreet to be precise.' He explained how they would walk on the meandering slopes of Longstreet, passing the bridge and walking down towards the Tea Plantations, admiring the vegetation past the bridge as you head toward Small Soppo. Dylan walked past my mother's house in Buea.

Later Dylan told me how he even took a trip with the Rapid Response Unit of the Cameroonian military and went deep into the once disputed territory between Cameroon and Nigeria, the very oil-rich Bakassi Peninsular. I could not believe what I was hearing. Yep, Dylan Moore, living in Newport, South Wales, was so influenced by the sights and sounds of the Mo-Ta-Sawa (the water people) that he proposed to his wife. Dylan and his wife have walked on my footprints.

I have known **Jude Emmanuel Kebuma Tita** almost all my life. Jude grew up in Down Road Small Soppo. His latest book on tithes (Blessed Hope, 2017) is available on Amazon. He has done a lot of research on the health benefits of *Gnetum africanum* or Eru Leaves as we call them in Cameroon. Jude stood with me during my darkest days in Small Soppo, for which I am forever grateful.

Mr **Efange Protus Esuka** I also knew growing up, his house borders that of my father, the disputed house that saw me leaving my village at such haste. I knew Mr Efange as a writer, Jude Emmanuel and I formed part of his choir group in the village as we were growing up. We entered a competition organised by the Cameroon Development Cooperation and made it to the quarter finals, we lost to a French group from Bastos in Yaoundé. I have always wondered about Mr Efange, I am very happy he decided to contribute to this anthology.

Mesue Lucy Ebude has the burning desire to become a writer, the way she speaks, her view of the world, her strong stance on women's rights.

When **Joffi Ewusi** heard I was in Cameroon, she travelled to Buea and visited me at our old house, she met my mother. Joffi hails from Great Soppo, a picturesque village at the foot of the Fako Mountain in Buea. She studied at the University of Buea and later moved to the University of Yaoundé 1 to read Commonwealth Studies for her first Master's degree, then Commonwealth and American Literary Studies for a second. She is a doctoral scholar at Yaoundé 1. She won the Eko Award for the Furtherance of Literature (prose category) for her novel *Christmas Carols in June*.

Kale Dante is on the brink of despair, yet clings onto the last mussel of hope. Poetic winds brought our path together, KD and I. We wrote and reciprocated each other's poetry from the distant lamentations of 'Indira', to the alluring charms of 'Farzana', we speak and talk of love and the hope of our generation which lies on our shoulders. We try not to despair even though 'the youth of today are our future' is not something that rings truly in our part of the world. Kale Dante is a friend. He is a Cameroonian poet, storyteller and a political analyst pursuing an MPA in the University of Gannon, in Erie, Pennsylvania, USA. A former student and youth leader, he was born and grew up in Buea, where he developed a love for literature at very young age from the fireside stories his dad told him, and his reading of the abundant folklore of traditional African literature. With a burning passion, Kale Dante fearlessly articulates issues of democracy, love, and the African identity. When I read Dante's poem 'My first white hair', I laughed, for in 2003 I wrote a poem published in *Between a Mountain and a Sea*, entitled 'Playing with your white hair (for Mr. Ndanga)': '… what greater love expressed from father to son / than playing with your white hair.' As you read and forge your way into Kale's psyche, hear the voice of a sage as he tries to pass wisdom to his, to my generation.

Dr **Hans Ndah Nyaa** I met during my second trip to Cameroon, he thought it was better to meet in his house because of the political upheavals in Cameroon. He is the brains behind Nyaa Publishing which is doing a great job in terms of giving Anglophone Cameroonians a voice. Mr Nyaa is softly spoken, and he was very keen on contributing to the anthology. He hails from Mbengwi in the Northwest Region of Cameroon. He holds a PhD from the University of Yaoundé 1. He is the winner of the 2013 EKO Literary Award for drama, has authored several plays, short stories, hymns and poetry collections. In addition to his job as a publisher, Nyaa presently teaches American Literature and Publishing at the University of Bamenda. I'm hoping the Nyaa publishing house can form a partnership with Hafan Books and Richard Davies of Parthian Books to carry on the bridge building project, the creative link between Wales and Cameroon.

As you read **Prudentia Binwi Asobo**'s story 'The *Tekumbeng* Parade' you will be seeing through the eyes of every Cameroonian. This ritual sends strong-hearted men to seek shelter far beyond the parading eyes of the Tekumbeng Women, mysterious middle-aged women, bare-chested carriers of ancient voodoo curses. Prudentia is a member of the Anglophone Cameroonian Writers Association, Yaoundé branch, she currently works at the Ministry of Education in the University of Yaoundé 1. She is a writer and critic, author of the poetry collections *In a Predicament All My Life* (2015), *Asomne Amwue Nda (Sorrow in the House)* (2016), and *Heroes in the Grave* (2017), among others.

I met **Julia Forster** at writing workshop organized by Wales PEN Cymru in Machynlleth. When the workshop was over, Julia introduced herself and signed a copy of her book *What a Way to Go*. Later she wrote an article for the BBC about my work. In a chapter in Julia's book, to show her dislike for her mother's new boyfriend, instead of defrosting some prawns by pouring boiled water onto them, or allowing them to thaw, she picks them up and one by one puts them into her mouth before putting them back in the bowl. In the background is Eddy Grant's song 'Gimme Hope, Joanna Gimme Hope'. (In one of the worse incidents in my life, in Pechatniki hostel in Moscow, I was taken hostage and almost beaten to death, hot knives placed on my body by about thirty Cameroonians, guess which music was playing in the background.) Julia and I are starting a collaboration next year looking into 'Rites of Passage'. She is an author of many books including *Muses*, *What a Way to Go*, and is currently working on *Saudade* based on a mysterious encounter, she confided in me.

Casia Wiliam is currently the Bardd Plant Cymru, Children's Poet Laureate for Wales. She invited me to take part at in Oxfam event at the Senedd, Cardiff National Assembly. When I published *Asylum* (Hafan Books, 2016), Casia bought ten copies on behalf of Oxfam. She is a passionate advocate for human rights and gender equality.

Kange Ernest is a soothsayer angered by the ongoing gentrification of his place of birth of Tole, where the Cameroon Development Cooperation has its Tea Plantation. I knew Kange as boy growing up in Small Soppo in Buea, he grew up in the suburbs of Tole, hence his lamentation as he witnessed the destruction of his place of birth. If anyone deserved a chance to play football for the Cameroonian national team it was Kange, he was a genius with the ball at his feet. Unfortunately, he had a terrible accident in Nigeria which ended his football ambitions. He now teaches drama at the Royalty Academy of Arts, Abuja, Nigeria.

Rudolph Elinge Kange weaves magic beyond the wisdom of his age, he has the potential to become a great writer.

Young **Collins Tometi** attended one of my workshops in Cameroon in August 2017.

Igbokwe Manka'a Mercy Ulomachi Shu is a women's rights activist, a writer, a fitness model and an entrepreneur. She has worked on projects designed to empower the girl child in countries such as Cameroon, Zanzibar Island, Tanzania and Nigeria. She is a contributing editor for an Afro-Pop culture magazine, *Face Magazine Nigeria*. To keep herself motivated, positive and in good form, she has adopted a lifestyle of keeping fit and eating clean. This lifestyle serves as an inspiration to others as she documents and shares her fitness journey online, sets up online fitness challenges and campaigns.

clare e. potter is a bilingual poet and performer, currently poet-in-residence in a medieval house in the Black Mountains of Wales. She has translated poems of Ifor ap Glyn and is widely published in the UK and USA. She was one of the writers selected to be a Hay Festival Writer at Work and thanks to a Literature Wales bursary, her second collection of poetry is forthcoming. She left teaching at Cardiff University to focus on working on collaborative community projects. She believes everyone has a story worth telling. Her MA was in Afro-Caribbean Literature at the University of Southern Mississippi, where her supervisor was Juliana Makuchi Nfah-Abbenyi – originally from Cameroon.

Johnson Eben Bisong is one of the writers I met at a meeting organized by the Anglophone Cameroonian Writers' Association in Yaoundé in December 2017. We have a lot in common, including the fact that we attended the same secondary school in Buea, GHS Bokwango. (Till this day, my mother does not know why I never finished at that school, the truth is, I was dismissed because of my absences when I was in form three going to form four. I just did not understand what the teachers were talking about.) Johnson is a talented dramatist, script writer, actor and musician. I remembered him very well, he prayed a nice Christian prayer, he is an evangelist with published works on Christian literature, he ended his prayers by asking the ancestors who brought me to Yaoundé to take me safely back to Wales; they did. As I sit down and read his poems, I imagine myself sitting next to a waterfall, listening to the wise words of an Ekulekule (tortoise).

The first time I visited Cameroon in August 2017, it took me about two weeks for my brain to adjust. So much so that by the time I felt comfortable to see people, I was preparing to travel back to Wales. I still could not bring myself to visit my father's family in Wonyalyonga, Buea Town. The one person I would have loved to meet there is **Ndumbe Lyonga La Manjinja**. Well, during my second visit I did meet the great man in his compound in the small village of Wondongor at the foot of Mount Cameroon, he had prepared 'Enderley Bread' (ground coco-yams, mixed vegetables, fish) and meat stew served with the sweetest of palm wine. I was accompanied on this journey by my niece Enanga, my nephew Collins, Palmer Ngalle Mbua my friend and brother on a technicality. Ngalle aka Pamol accompanied me to my father's family home, I needed a friendly reassurance. (Ngalle is a great film producer, director and writer. He is currently working on a script about the Great Chief Kuva of the Bakweri people. I am writing a poem to support the script for I truly believe Kuva is currently being strangled by his coffin.) We danced the traditional dance, Ndumbe poured libations and summoned the gods of our ancestors, he invited some of the youth (he runs a project that promotes the

Bakweri language and empowers the youth). That day we played the Djembe loud and danced. That is how we spent the first day of 2018.

Ndumbe Lyonga La Manjinja is a writer and storyteller, currently working on a collection of stories, a short play and a book, *The White Man of Africa*. His contribution in this anthology, 'Nene', a short story, speaks of domestic abuse which is endemic in my society. For such a young head, Ndumbe is full of wisdom, he enjoys telling 'maitos' (ancient proverbs), he speaks Bakweri so fluently it was as if he was with the gods when they passed that knowledge to the Bakweri people.

Des Mannay's writing is 'focused on hard-hitting social issues, poems which make a statement' (*Sabotage Reviews*). I first met Mr Mannay, aka hooliganpoet, during the Hub Festival at a tapas bar in Westgate Street, Cardiff. It was as if we knew one another a long time ago. Des Mannay is prolific in the literary scene and has won several competitions such as the 'rethinkyourmind' poetry competition (2015) or runner-up and highly commended in the Disability Arts Cymru Poetry Competition (2015).

I first met **Aliya Kaaba** during a poetry and spoken word event called 'Where I'm Coming From', organised by poet Hanan Issa at the Tramshed in Grangetown, Cardiff. When Aliya was reading her piece, I had goosebumps. She is the founder of Just AK, an ethical streetwear brand. She is a clinical scientist and still dabbles in clinical work from time to time. Her passion for writing poems and short stories began after completing the 'NaNoWriMo' competition in 2016. Since then Aliya has been using the power of written words to express what life is like as a black, Muslim female living in the UK. Like her t-shirt designs, her written work will make you think and question society.

Also at the 'Where I'm Coming From' event I heard **Suryatapa Mukherjee** read out a poem about her complicated relationship with her father: 'He grew up with a strange sort of evil / Which is unleashed at home; / And outside, its face is charity.' I am happy she is sharing this poem with you, for truly the poem touched my soul, she touched my soul. Her work has been published on Medium, Breakthrough India, The F-Word and more. She is now working with the Iris Prize Film Festival. During her MA in International Journalism, she covered the Israel-Palestine conflict, the Syrian refugee crisis, LGBT+ rights in Jordan and student immigration in the UK. She has been interviewed for a series on bisexuality in India, which led to the UN including bisexual content in their global charter on LGBT+ rights. You can find her Political Personal channel on YouTube, with 'Sue Thinks Aloud' – a vlog series with a satirical take on racism.

Joyce Ashuntantang is a poet, actress, creative writer and Associate Professor of English at the University of Hartford, USA. She has appeared as an invited poet in many countries around the world and has contributed to nine international anthologies of poetry including *Reflections: An Anthology of New Work by African Women Poets* (2013) and *We Have Crossed Many Rivers. New Poetry from Africa* (2012). A graduate of three continents, she received a BA in English with a minor in Theater Arts from the University of Yaoundé, Cameroon, a Masters in Library and Inform-ation science from University of Aberystwyth, Wales, UK, and a PhD in English/African Literature from the City University of New York. Her poems have been translated into Spanish, Greek, Hebrew, Turkish and Bangla.

When I was in Cameroon for the first time in August 2017, not knowing how I was going to introduce myself to the Cameroonian literati and to the nation, to tell them of my work and why I was in Cameroon, I decided to visit the Ministry of Arts and Culture. Seeing a minister in Cameroon is not an easy task, it is not like walking into the surgery of Julie Morgan in Whitchurch. At the minister's office I introduced myself to the secretary, who told me, and I quote, 'the minister is having his afternoon nap'. I completely understood, my gosh I was so hot, given the perfect temperature at the minister's office, I too would have retired for a nap. The secretary asked me to wait at the reception. As I waited three women walked in, one of them without any hesitation asked my name and what I was doing at the Ministry of Arts and Culture. As the conversation flowed, she introduced herself as Becky Tchonko Bissong, and as it turns out, Becky is a senior journalist at CRTV (Cameroon Radio Television), she is a mother, a gender advocate, a gospel artist, and she is also Head of Projects at MEWIC (Media Women Imparting Change). Becky had come to see the minister to obtain permission to do some filming in Bamenda. She gave me five telephone numbers, one of them belonged to one Mr Charles Tembei, a senior journalist and the host of 'Literary Half Hour', a CRTV radio programme with an audience of over eight million. I did an impromptu interview with Becky at the minister's reception area, by the time she left I'd forgotten why I was there in the first place. It had become unnecessary for me to see the minister.

I telephoned Charles Tembei and left him a voice mail. I then travelled on coach for six hours to Tiko for my creative writing workshop, where I spoke about Hedd Wyn the soldier poet, the Black Chair, the battle of Passchendaele, the Eisteddfod of 1917 and the pointlessness of wars. Later that evening Charles Tembei called me. Back in Yaoundé the next day I met him at his office in CRTV. It was as if I had met my long-lost brother. I sat down with Mr Charles and recorded a programme that was broadcast across Cameroon. When we finished two hours later, Mr Charles (whose nickname is 'Different Levels of Intensities') shook my hand and said: 'Ngalle, the gods of your ancestors have remembered your name, you are no longer a molikilikili (stick insect) you are now a njorku (an elephant).' I must confess I have nothing against the molikilikili.

This is how I was introduced to Cameroon, and the Cameroonian literati. When I went back in December for the South West Cultural Festival, I spent five days with Charles and his family in their beautiful house in Yaoundé. Charles told me a story about his father, Pa Joe, and Charles's wife: how Pa Joe made her to walk for miles carrying two bunches of plantains on her head. When she asked how far they were going to walk, Pa Joe simply said: 'We are only going around the corner'. He insisted on stopping and greeting all the extended family in the neighbouring villages, as you do. Charles's wife was tired but 'who was she' to tell the father-in-law. They reached their destination three hours later, and she did not talk to Charles until they got back to Yaoundé. We all laughed as we enjoyed breakfast in Charles's family home.

As you get ready to start reading from the various contributors, I also want to reach out to a musician whose work has provided me solace, deep peace, strength and inspiration. Steve Eaves is a Welsh poet, songwriter and singer, working in the Welsh language. He has lived for most of his life in the Bangor area of North Wales. He has been a performing musician for over 45 years. At the end of the Gwyl Arall Festival in Caernarfon in 2016, at the finale of the festival he and his band played a song called 'Nos Da Mam' (Good night mam). At first, I just sat and listened without understanding the lyrics. When they finished the audience pleaded for them to play the song again. This time around Bethan, Ifor's wife, translated the lyrics for me. As she translated she cried. We sang the chorus together, as we sang it took me back to one of the first poems I wrote when I came to Wales: 'Au revoir'. I was terrified of never seeing my mother again:

(…) She hugged me still avoiding my gaze
then she took my hands into hers
and slowly but steadily
she gave each of my fingers a gently bite

paying tribute to an old village adage
knotting and sealing the fact that
as I struggle to climb
the thoughts and prayers
my relatives would be with me
as mine would be with them (…)

As you read each piece, I can only hope it acts as a small guide into Wales and Cameroon. Back in 2009, in his book *The Catholic Orangemen of Togo and other Conflicts I Have Known*, former British Ambassador Craig Murray described Cameroon as 'God's gift to mankind'. Looking at media reports today, one wouldn't think so. May the contributions of the Cameroonian writers bring you a taste, a smell, a feel of what Cameroon is, even though the two elephants are sizing one another up, pacing up and down the virgin terrain.

Forgive me if I am unable to write the biographies of every contributor to this anthology, I have not met every single one, though I hope to meet them one day.

I once organised a poetry event at the Miller's Tavern in Riverside, Cardiff in 2004, and Grahame Davies was in the audience, I asked, and he gave me his permission to read out his poem 'Rough Guide', so I hope you don't mind if I start this anthology with this poem. In Russia I was called all kind of names, from 'churnie abyzian' (black monkey) to 'churnie joppa' (black ass). I was a minority even at the Cameroonian embassy, there I was a Nigerian. I have been a nomad everywhere apart from here in Wales, here I am a Black African, in some quarters I am a 'Refugee Writer', in some a Writer, Poet and Playwright, to some I am just a Cameroonian. When we travelled to Port Talbot with my Ely football team, Avenue Hotspurs, I was taunted on the sidelines with names like 'blackie', hahahahaha. Chaiii! one has seen all sorts under the heavens. As you read Grahame's poem, you pick up a map of the world and visit those different cities, you find yourself being called different names, Black, Navaho, Cajun, Palestinian. 'Nice city. Now where's the ghetto?' As I told my daughter Jolie about this anthology project and read out the poem 'Rough Guide' to her, she interrupted me and said, 'Dad, do you mean *the* Grahame Davies, the Bard?' 'Yes, Mbando,' I answered. My daughter shouted: 'O my days, dad, we're deconstructing Grahame Davies's poem 'Lerpwl' and studying it for Welsh A-level!' When Jolie was three years old, we visited Grahame, now she is sixteen. I wonder if Grahame would recognise her. We decided to visit Grahame at his house in Cathedral Road.

Grahame Davies

Rough Guide

It happens inevitably,
Like water finding its level:
Every time I open a travel book,
I sail past the capital cities, the sights,
And dive straight into the backstreets of the index
To find that in France, I'm Breton,
In New Zealand, I am Maori;
In the USA-depending on which part-
I'm Navaho, Cajun, or black.

I'm the Wandering Welshman.
I'm Jewish everywhere.
Except, of course, in Israel.
There, I am Palestinian.
It's some kind of complex, I know,
That makes me pick this scab on my psyche.
I wonder sometimes what it would be like
To go to these places
And just enjoy.
No, as I wonder the continents of the guidebooks,
Whatever chapter maybe my destination,
The question's always the same when I arrive:
'Nice city. Now where's the ghetto?'

Ifor ap Glyn

Six Poems

CAERDYDD 3.6.17

*(Pan ddaeth Real a Juve i'n prifddinas ar gyfer rownd derfynol
Cynghrair y Pencampwyr, am un noson roedd Caerdydd fel
prifddinas Ewrop.)*

Sarete sempre
i nostri fratelli e sorelle europei
Siaradwn â'n gilydd
mewn lliwiau gwahanol,
a rhwng banllefau'r soseri,
cymeradwyaeth cwpanau
a hisian stêm llond stadiwm,
mae ein dinas
fel caffi cyfandir cyfan.
A'n lleisiau fel tyllau haul
mewn coedwig tywyll…
Siempre seréis
nuestros hermanos y hermanas europeos
mae'n croeso ni yma, yn aros 'run fath…

CARDIFF 3.6.17

(When Real and Juve came to contest the Champions League final,
for one night, Cardiff was the capital of Europe)

Sarete sempre
i nostri fratelli e sorelle europei
We talk to each other
in different colours,
and what with the applause of saucers,
the acclamation of cups,
and the steam hiss of a full stadium,
our city
is café to a whole continent!
And our voices are like sun-lit holes
In the dark of the forest…
Siempre seréis
nuestros hermanos y hermanas europeos
here, our *croeso* remains constant…

Y TŶ HWN

'If we want Wales, we will have to make Wales'
– Gwyn Alf Williams

Daeth gwanwyn yn hwyr i'n gwlad;
y gaea wedi cloi ein huchelgais
a gwydro ein dyheadau,
cyn y dadmer mawr,
a barodd i'r gwteri garglo
a'r landeri garlamu.

Boed felly, haul, ar y tŷ hwn heddiw;
dyma bair ein dadeni; a llwyfan i'n llais;
lle canwn ein gweledigaeth i fodolaeth...

A down yma o sawl cwmwd, megis cynt –
wrth droedio'r llwybr dreiniog cul
sydd â gwlan fel trimins Dolig ar ei hyd;
neu wrth heidio lawr y lôn wleb
sy'n ddrych i sglein yr awyr –
down yma, i gyffwrdd â'r gorwel
a'i blygu at iws gwlad.

Ac wrth ddynesu
o'n cymoedd a'n mynyddoedd
at ein dinas barhaus,

diolchwn nad oes tyllau bwledi
ym mhileri'r tŷ hwn,
dim ond cwmwl tystion wrth ein cefn
ym mhob plwraliaeth barn.

Ac wrth gael ein tywys
i gynteddau'r tŷ,
boed angerdd i'n trafod
a phwyll ymhob cymod;

boed i anodd ddod yn syml,
a'r heriol ddod yn hwyl;
a boed i ni gofio'r wireb hon beunydd:
'cynt y cyferfydd dau ddyn
na dau fynydd'

THIS HOUSE

*Commissioned to celebrate the opening of the new session of the
Welsh Parliament in June 2016.*

> *'If we want Wales, we will have to make Wales'*
> *— Gwyn Alf Williams*

Spring came late to our country;
the winter locked down ambition
and put our aspirations on ice,
before the big thaw
which made the drains gargle
and the downpipes gush.

And so, may the sun shine bright on this house today;
This cauldron of our rebirth; the platform for our voice,
where we sing our vision into being . . .

We come here from many commotes, as before –
treading the overgrown path, barbed
with wool like Christmas trimmings;
and crowding down the wet lane
which mirrors the sky's shine –
we come here, to touch the horizon
and bend it for common good.
And as we,
from our valleys and mountains,
approach our perpetual city,

we give thanks there are no bullet holes
in the pillars of this house,
just a cloud of witnesses
who'll maintain us in all manner of beliefs.

And as we are led
to the halls of this house,
may there be passion in our debate;
prudence in conciliation;

let 'difficult' become simple, and 'challenging' become
          fun;
and let us each day repeat these maxims:
that 'sooner will two men come together
than two mountains.'

PEBLIG: 87.4%

Sdim gorwel yma; dim ond toeau gwâr
yn cau'n gwlwm amdanom;
cylchoedd gwm cnoi
yn fydysawd sêr dan draed;

a phwy a ŵyr na chawn ni ddinas`barhaus
yma, lle mae'r ffenestri mor ddall â'r dyfodol,

yma, lle mae waliau brics fy mebyd,
na fedr ond un iaith eu codi;

yma, lle mae'r camerâu yn syllu'n slei
o ben eu polion, o gyrion ein gwyll?

There's no horizon here; just rooftops
closing in a knot around us;
chewing-gum circles
form a universe of stars underfoot;

and who's to say we won't found our citadel
here, where the windows are blind as our future,

here, where the brick walls of my youth
still stand, built in one language alone;

here, where the cameras surreptitiously survey
from their pole tops, the edges of our darkness?

MEDI 1917

*(ar ganmlwyddiant cadeirio Hedd Wyn
a seremoni ail-agor yr Ysgwrn, 6.9.2017)*

Am na ddeuai nôl
o'r llaid i'r Beudy Llwyd,
ni safai a'i bicwarch yn ei law,
gan hel y gwair yn gawod haul
i mewn drwy'r drws ucha.

Ni safai rhwng y pileri chwaith
ynghanol llwch a gwres
gan weithio awdl drom o das,
na chribo'i hochrau'n dwt at y gaea.

A gydol y dyddiau byrion hynny,
ni fyddai'n mynd at fanc yr haf
er mwyn porthi'r gwartheg ar jaen;
ni welai'r tarth yn codi o'u cyrff,
na'u hanadl yn blodeuo'n y gwyll.

Ac am na ddeuai ef yn ôl,
ni cherddai byth i fyny i'r tŷ,
lle roedd cadair wag
yn ei hir-ddisgwyl;
er iddo fydylu'i gerddi ar hyd y caeau hyn.

Ac oni rhyfeddai heddiw,
o weld cynifer yn dod heb bladur
at eu cynhaeaf nhw?
Yn hel o gymdogaeth ehangach
rhwng gwydr y waliau hyn

a'r byrddau te,
i yfed o'r un olygfa,
ac i ymdeimlo â'r absenoldeb
sy'n llafar ar hyd y lle?

HARVEST 1917

*(On the hundredth anniversary of the posthumous chairing of the
poet Hedd Wyn, killed in World War One, and to celebrate the
reopening of his home to the public, 6.9.2017)*

Because he would never come back
from the mud to this grey byre
he would not stand fork in hand,
pitching the hay through the upper door
like a shower of sun;

he would not stand between these posts
amidst the heat and dust,
fashioning the rick like a weighty ode,
raking its sides ready for winter.

And throughout those shortened days
he would not dip into the summer he'd banked,
to feed the cows chained here,
nor see the warm mist rise from their flanks,
their breath like flowers in the dark.

And because he would not come back,
he would never walk up to the house

where an empty chair long awaited him,
although he'd stooked his poems
across these fields.

And wouldn't he marvel this day,
to see so many coming without scythes, to their
harvest,
gathering from a wider world
between the cafe tables and walls of glass
to drink the same view
and sense his absence
that still calls, through each and every blade of grass..

CAMP OBAMA

(Louisiana 2008)

Wedi p'nawn hir yn rhyfeddu'n swrth
at y plastai mawrion â'r colofnau gwynion,
(beddrodau cyfoeth yn llygad yr haul),

Daeth niwl ar lannau'r Mississippi gyda'r hwyr,
Y pontydd fel ysbrydion pell
a'r arwyddion neon yn nofio,
wedi gollwng angor o'r strydoedd islaw...

Ac ar y teledu, yn ôl yn y gwesty,
daeth hud ar genedl gyfan
ac ymgollais yn y jiwbili fawr
wrth i ddyn o'r hen gyfandir
gynnig ei obeithion powld
i genedl gyfan gyndyn
o wynion a chyngaethion...

Ond ar sianel arall,
yng nghannwyll llygad rhyw stadiwm bêl-droed
gwelais gewri duon
yn hyt-hyt-hyrddio'n chwyrn i'w gilydd,
ac enwau fy hil innau,
yn Evans a Griffiths a Davis a Jones
yn warthnod ar eu gwarrau llydan...

A phan gwyd yr hud, pan dawdd y niwl,
camp i'r mab darogan hwn
roi cnawd am esgyrn etholiad,
chwythu anadl i'r gobeithion powld,

ac impio croen yfory
ar greithiau ddoe...

...ond gwn y bydd yn cerdded
â breuddwydion sawl gwlad
yn cynnal ei draed,
a'n hewyllys yn llusern ar ei lwybr.

SON OF PROPHECY

(for Barack Obama)

After a long afternoon marveling drowsily
at the white columned mansions,
the whitéd sepulchres of wealth
beneath the staring sun,
evening brought mist
to the Missisippi townships;
bridges like distant ghosts...
and the neon signs swam,
slipping anchor from the streets below...

And on TV, back at the hotel,
a whole nation was under a spell
and I celebrated with them
this new jubilee,
as a man from the dark continent
offered his audacious hopes,

to an uneasy one-nation audience
of whites and former slaves.

On another channel
I saw a storm of black giants
     in the very eye of a new stadium,
hut-hut-hurling themselves at each other,
and the names of *our* nation,
Evans and Griffiths and Davis and Jones
on the broad shoulders of our "brothers"
branding our shame ...

And what a feat it will be,
for this son of prophecy
to put flesh on the bones of election,
breathe life into bold hopes
and to graft tomorrow's skin
over the scars of yesterday
when the magic of the mist melts away...

DIWRNOD YN KAMPALA – BECHGYN Y STRYD

(Gyda blwyddyn 6 Ysgol Gymraeg Aberystwyth)

Yng nghornel iard y rheilffordd
cysga'r bechgyn mewn papur newydd llipa
fel anrhegion blêr i ddiwrnod arall,
yn gwingo'n y gwyll ar waelod hen wagen
a'u cefnau'n dost.

Mwg o'r trenau
ac olwynion ar gledrau sy'n eu deffro.
Stretsio.
Oglau chwys o gesail.
Golchi ceg hefo dŵr rhydlyd
o danc injan stêm.

Brysio gyda'r haul newydd
at ruthr y farchnad.
Gorymdaith loriau'n troi'n dagfa draffig.
Goleuadau coch. Brecio'n swnllyd.
Bananas yn disgyn
yn glewt o gefn lori.

A'r bechgyn
fel piod
yn cipio'r trysor melys i'w gwerthu,

gan gadw llygad barcud
am yrrwyr lori blin,
y cwsmeriaid prin
a gelynion y gyfraith.

Weithiau rhaid ffoi rhag yr heddlu,

rhag cael eu curo,
rhag cael eu carcharu dros dro;
a bydd lliwiau'r farchnad yn blyrio i gyd
wrth wibio bant fel wildebeest,
a llwch y stryd yn diflannu dan draed.

Wrth iddi nosi,
gall y bechgyn bori'n ddiogel
ar reis, matoke neu cassava, 1
ac os bydd llond poced o elw'r dydd,
gallant fwyta cig,
â blas buddugoliaeth
yn tynnu dŵr o'r dannedd.

A chyn cysgu,
rhaid lapio'u hunain eto
fel anrhegion i'w postio
at yfory …

ONE DAY IN KAMPALA – THE STREET BOYS

(with year 6 students from Ysgol Gymraeg Aberystwyth)

In the corner of the railway yard
The boys sleep in old newspapers
Like badly wrapped presents for a new day
Wincing on the floor of the railway wagon
Their backs stiff in the new dawn.
Wheels on rails and steam from the trains rouse them.
They stretch.
Sniff armpit sweat,
Rinse their mouths with rusty water
From an engine's water tank.
They hurry in the new sun
To the bustle of the market,
The procession of lorries held in traffic
Red lights. Brake screech.
Bananas fall with a clump
From the tailgate

And the boys like magpies,
seize the sweet treasure to sell,
Keeping a hawk-eye open
For irate lorry drivers,
reluctant customers,
And their enemies from the law.

Sometimes they have to flee from the police,
So as not to be beaten
So as not to be locked up;
And the colours of the market become a blur

as they leap away like wildebeest,
The street dust disappears beneath their feet.

And when night comes
The boys can snack safely
on rice, matoke or cassava,
and if they have a pocketful of the day's proceeds
they eat meat,
it makes their mouths water
and tastes of victory.

Before they sleep
They wrap themselves again
Like presents to be posted
To an untrustworthy tomorrow ...

Adeola Dewis

Route2Roots

Awa o s'oro ile wa o
Awa o s'oro ile wa o

Awa o s'oro ile wa o
Awa o s'oro ile wa o
Esin kan o pe, o ye
Esin kan o pe kawa ma s'oro
Awa o s'oro ile wa o

We are here, right?
A continuation of them
Those that have gone before
Black skins and sweat
The aftertaste of our everyday
Their blood in the crevices of our gums,
Their blood running through
The way we walk and talk, the way we laugh and
        move and sit
Look at that hand on her hip

It's in our DNA Dele say...

Invocations to North and South
Turning East and West and yes
We know what it feels like
To lift our hands to the sky and bow down to the earth
Reverent, we know we know, we know
That feeling of wanting to connect
To something...

But we forget
Is it 500 years now?

And so how we say
Ade-ola
Yemonja
Ogun, Shango and the orisha

Not making excuses for why we doh say it so
It's in our Caribbean lingo
This Caribbean becoming
Constant becoming
Not saying sorry
For why we say it so
It's in our Caribbean 'becoming'
Our re-membering
Treasuring
Performing
Fragments

And no, doh apologise
Is okay
These words, we can learn and re-learn
But when we perform these fragments
Yuh doh find it feel nice so?

Touching something real that Camille and Marvin say
moves beyond
Translation

And is true
That we own more water than land
And on the I-land of

Sun, sea and sand
Navel strings and ancient indigenous bones

We know
We have **in** those Ocean graves
Restless ancestors

Ifa, Ori, Jah know
We feelin' the feeling
Pregnant with loss
Depletion,
Amnesia

Eee
Ira wa, ira wa-o
Eee ira wa, ira wa-o
Ko-je ki'rin wa sure dilogun o
A di lo jo lo ge li jo ira wa

How a generation looking go see?

And re-member?
If our members are happy to be free
From
Old

We know we are new
And not so new too
Standing on shoulders with deep roots
More unseen than visible

Dancing like Douen
Moving forwards with footprints looking back

A generation looking go see

A generation seeing go feel
Legacy
Music, magic, beauty
Power, knowledge and
Journeys across seas
Resistance
Spreading wings

Like Amé

Flying back home

Making in this gayelle
Earth Science and music
With power like Moko Jumbie

Mama D'lo
Mama Osun
Mama Dantor
And

Me.

Douglas Achingale

Six Poems

GONE BUT STILL ON

It's like only yesterday
But eleven winding years
Have wistfully whirled away
Since the legendary gadfly
Violently hopped the twig

A pathos-ridden untimely exit
Of a perfect boon companion
Dry-throated he left us
Of his daily stage calisthenics
Of his sweet tub-thumping prolixity

But only the flesh is gone
The spirit is still on…
For the wily Obassinjom Warrior
Is omnipresent in his prescient scribbles
Scribbles pervaded by angst

Yes, the most-cruel death
Of the talkative BB
A literary beast
Mourned by our nation
No requiem yet for you
(Last) virulent writer

THE HONOURABLE MINISTER

Hey, don't run away,
Honourable Mr. Minister of State!
The land bleeds, your valise sips
And there you are at the terminus
Of the border town, set to sail

The valise is full of treasure
The treasure of the land
The sweat of the people
Apparently full and heavy
It seems to say:
"Let me fall, I won't go with you!"

But Honourable Mr. Minister marches on
With steady serenity and surpassing aplomb
Load in hand, towards the ostentatious boat
Bound for Switzerland

O, how a million toiling men's labour
Fills the coffers of one gargantuan soul!
O, how the land is sucked dry
Whereas men toil and cry!
O, how foreign markets blossom in effulgence
While ours gropes in blinding somberness!
O, how he carves his strides
Towards the sumptuous Swiss boat!

Come back, merciless hawk!
Turn back your strides, unruly turtle
That eats his fellows' eggs!
Sea goddess, o mighty thee,

Bar his way! Cast off his scrotum!

And all about him is odious, I swear
This Honourable Mr. Minister of State
It seems the hair is deciduous
That caps his piggish head
His abdomen is an enormous mass
Huge as the carcass of a ful-fed hog
His legs more scanty of flesh
Than the antennae of a cockroach

Ah, his breath stinks, dear me!
Like the whiffy stench of fart
Emanating from under a blanket!
This Honourable Mr. Minister of State!

I WANT TO GO

I am at the end of my tether
time for me to break free
from this land of milk and honey -
cum-land of niff very dingy

I am wrapped in awful tedium
high time I left this promise land
now sprinkled with giant thorns,
strewn with banana peelings

I am distressed ad nauseam
I must leave this land of glory
now teetering on the brink
of total, irreversible collapse

You who choose to stay back
the acrid smell will
suffocate you at short notice
the obscurity will blind you forever

Since you don't want to leave
weep not when gigantic thorns
kiss your tender soles
when the peelings render you lame

To insist to remain here
is eloquent pointer to one truth:
that your doleful preference
is to collapse with the land

LOST HAPPINESS

I rose from my mat
With pains in my ribs
A hole in my stomach
From forced fasting

I toddled off down street
No destination in mind
But with a vague hope
To find a giving hand

I came across a bin
With a half stale morsel
I settled for it
Near a tall tiled house

I peeped through the curtain
I saw a po-faced man
Roast fish in his plate
But who could not munch

I eyed a tight-lipped dame
In a marbled bed
With a thick soft mattress
But who could not sleep

I thought of my mat
My usual deep sleep
Plus the food in my hand
Which I so much relished

I knocked at the door
And there emerged the bloke

"Why wouldn't you eat?
Why would your dame not sleep?"

I heard him mumble:
"Are we really to blame?
No gunshots around
But bullet wounds in our mind"

I eyed the house again
I went quietly away
My stale chunk in my hand
To munch and slumber deep

QUESTIONS TO THE BARONS

When I quizzed the Barons
I was entombed alive
In this wicked cell
Like the miserable flea
That goes subterranean with the corpse

I asked the Barons
Of what use are the mega-bucks
From our abundant oil
If the bucks cannot smooth the road
Leading to the oil source

I questioned the Barons
Why uniformed scallywags
Have fat monthly packages
While avid workaholics
Merely eke out a living

I sought to know
From the Barons
Why many ostentatious miscreants
Go off gallivanting around
Whereas a select few
Stay handcuffed like me

I asked the Barons
Why some prestigious rascals
With no known monthly income
Use innocent taxpayers' sweat
To finance their charity works

I questioned the Barons
Why there is never talk
Of resource scarcity
When they want to indulge
In their wasteful activities
But often talk of scarcity
When we want to do things
For our common good

Just because I sought answers
To those searching question
I was apprehended, manacled
Entombed alive in this wicked cell
A cell wherein the Barons
Should rather dwell

WHITE-COLLAR LUNATICS

A yawning, capacious gap
 Separates them from those
Filthy street wanderers who forage
 For scraps and sleeping rough

 At the corporeal level, yes:
Corporal and sartorial elegance
 But upstairs they are
Like perfectly identical twins

They seem ever sloshed
 By Bacchus' sweet swizzle
Or under the potent influence
 Of some unkind 'baccy'

 Otherwise why would they
Treat us the rank and file
 As though we were rats and flies?
If lunacy from you
 Is distant, why crush comrades
Who catapulted you to the cockpit?

 The street wanderers
Are irretrievably mental
 But retrievable you are
From little self-effort

Up from your Van Winkle sleep!
 Arise! Arise! Arise!
Lest your today's hubris
 Will be your tomorrow's nemesis

Johnson Eben Bisong

Six Poems

THE BRIGHT STAR

'Twas noontide of summer,
 And mid-time of night;
And stars, in their orbits,
 Shone pale, thro' the light
Of the brighter, cold moon,
 'Mid planets her slaves,
Herself in the Heavens,
 Her beam on the waves.
I gazed awhile
 On her cold smile;
Too cold – too cold for me –
 There pass'd, as a shroud,
A fleecy cloud,
 And I turned away to thee,
Proud Evening Star,
 In thy glory afar,
And dearer thy beam shall be;
 For joy to my heart
Is the proud part
 Thou bearest in Heaven at night,
And more I admire
 Thy distant fire,
Than that colder, lowly light.

HAPPIEST DAAAAY

The happiest day -- the happiest hour
My sear'd and blighted heart hath known,
The highest hope of pride and power,
I feel hath flown.

Of power! said I? yes! such I ween;
But they have vanish'd long, alas!
The visions of my youth have been-
But let them pass.

And, pride, what have I now with thee?
Another brow may even inherit
The venom thou hast pour'd on me
Be still, my spirit!

The happiest day – the happiest hour
Mine eyes shall see – have ever seen,
The brightest glance of pride and power,
I feel – have been:

But were that hope of pride and power
Now offer'd with the pain
 Even then I felt -- that brightest hour
I would not live again:

For on its wing was dark alloy,
And, as it flutter'd – fell
An essence – powerful to destroy
A soul that knew it well.

In spring of youth it was my lot
To haunt of the wide world a spot

The which I could not love the less –
So lovely was the loneliness
Of a wild lake, with black rock bound,
And the tall pines that towered around.

But when the Night had thrown her pall
Upon that spot, as upon all,
And the mystic wind went by
Murmuring in melody –
Then – ah then I would awake
To the terror of the lone lake.

Yet that terror was not fright,
But a tremulous delight-
A feeling not the jeweled mine
Could teach or bribe me to define –
Nor Love – although the Love were thine.

Death was in that poisonous wave,
And in its gulf a fitting grave
For him who thence could solace bring
To his lone imagining –
Whose solitary soul could make
An Eden of that dim lake.

YOU ARE THE ONE

You are like me, you will die too, but not today:
you, incommensurate, therefore the hours shine:
if I say to you "To you I say," you have not been
set to music, or broadcast live on the ghost
radio, may never be an oil painting or
Old Master's charcoal sketch: you are
a concordance of person, number, voice,
and place, strawberries spread through your name
as if it were budding shrubs, how you remind me
of some spring, the waters as cool and clear
(late rain clings to your leaves, shaken by light wind),
which is where you occur in grassy moonlight:
and you are a lily, an aster, white trillium
or viburnum, by all rights mine, white star
in the meadow sky, the snow still arriving
from its earthwards journeys, here where there is
no snow (I dreamed the snow was you,
when there was snow), you are my right,
have come to be my night (your body takes on
the dimensions of sleep, the shape of sleep
becomes you): and you fall from the sky
with several flowers, words spill from your mouth
in waves, your lips taste like the sea, salt-sweet (trees
and seas have flown away, I call it
loving you): home is nowhere, therefore you,
a kind of dwell and welcome, song after all,
and free of any Eden we can name.

HE HAS NO NAMES

You have changed me already. I am a fireball
That is hurtling towards the sky to where you are
You can choose not to look up, but I am a giant orange ball
That is throwing sparks upon your face
Oh, look at them shake
Upon you like a great planet that has been murdered
      by change
O too this is so dramatic this shaking
Of my great planet that is bigger than you thought it
      would be
So, you ran and hid
Under a large tree. She was graceful, I think
That tree although soon she will wither
Into ten black snakes upon your throat
And when she does I will be wandering as I always am
A graceful lady that is part museum
Of the voices of the universe everyone else forgets
I will hold your voice in a little box
And when you come upon me I won't look back at you
You will feel a hand upon your heart while I place your
      voice back
Into the heart from where it came from
And I will not cry also
Although you will expect me to
I was wiser too than you had expected
For I knew all along you were mine

I FEEL YOUR PAINS

I gave you sorrow to hang on your wall
Like a calendar in one color.
I wear a torn place on my sleeve.
It isn't as simple as that.

Between no place of mine and no place of yours
You'd have thought I'd know the way by now
Just from thinking it over.
Oh, I know
I've no excuse to be stuck here turning
Like a mirror on a string,
Except it's hardly credible how
It all keeps changing.
Loss has a wider choice of directions
Than the other thing.

As if I had a system
I shuffle among the lies
Turning them over, if only
I could be sure what I'd lost.
I uncover my footprints, I
Poke them till the eyes open.
They don't recall what it looked like.
When was I using it last?
Was it like a ring or a light
Or the autumn pond
Which chokes and glitters but
Grows colder?
It could be all in the mind. Anyway
Nothing seems to bring it back to me.

And I've been to see
Your hands as trees borne away on a flood,
The same film over and over,
And an old one at that, shattering its account
To the last of the digits, and nothing
And the blank end.

The lightning has shown me the scars of the future.

I've had a long look at someone
Alone like a key in a lock
Without what it takes to turn.

It isn't as simple as that.

Winter will think back to your lit harvest
For which there is no help, and the seed
Of eloquence will open its wings
When you are gone.
But at this moment
When the nails are kissing the fingers good-bye
And my only
Chance is bleeding from me,
When my one chance is bleeding,
For speaking either truth or comfort
I have no more tongue than a wound.

I WILL OPEN THE DOOR

Our embrace lasted too long.
We loved right down to the bone.
I hear the bones grind, I see
our two skeletons.

Now I am waiting
till you leave, till
the clatter of your shoes
is heard no more. Now, silence.

Tonight, I am going to sleep alone
on the bedclothes of purity.
Aloneness
is the first hygienic measure.
Aloneness
will enlarge the walls of the room,
I will open the window
and the large, frosty air will enter,
healthy as tragedy.
Human thoughts will enter
and human concerns,
misfortune of others, saintliness of others.
They will converse softly and sternly.

Do not come anymore.
I am an animal
Very rarely.

Des Mannay

Three Poems

WALLET

I wish I could find
a wallet
on the floor.
Just like ones
I found before –
because my back
is up against
a wall.

I look for coins
on pavements,
in the gutter.
Too desperate to
look up at the sky.

I see fag-butts
at the fag end
of the day.
When I used to smoke,
I'd pick them up,
make a –
match thin –
Borstal cigarette.

Now I look
for wallets,
alongside

parked cars
because my need
is greater than
all yours.

I wish I'd thought
like this
a week ago –
when I found
one abandoned
near a pub
Instead I
meekly hand it in

Now I walk
past that pub
In case misfortune –
like lightning –
strikes again,
lightens
my own load.
Now I have
more mouths to
feed than me

A landlord shout –
stops me in my tracks!
Beckons me inside
I'm taken aback!

Here within –
a place I can't afford.
Then he says

the magic word, "Reward!".

A wad of –
rolled up £5 notes,
and it brings
a lump into my throat.

Lifted up –
the dark clouds of my mood,
and I hurried
Home! With drink and food –

THEY CALL ME

They call me Atticus
'coz I live in an attic

They call me Platypus
because I duck my bills

They call me often
until they've had their fill

They call me sicknote
because I'm often ill

They call me a cab

but never pay the meter

They call me 'Mr Loverman'
but hope I'll never meet her

They call me an alien
though I'm not from outer space

They call me 'Johnnie foreigner'
although I'm from this place

They call me wildcat
when I go on strike

They sound like Norman Tebbit
when they say, "On yer bike!"

They call me Ivan
when I've an awful cough

They call me a dosser
when I'm sleeping rough

All the things they call me
won't catch me when I fall

I'd prefer they didn't
call me anything at all

ON THE DEATH OF MUHAMMAD ALI

Goodbye butterfly
You stung like a bee
You stung me!
From you I learnt
resistance!
To all the
'nigger, nigger –
pull the trigger'
playground taunts
I could reply –
'C'mon Bugner!'

The kids at school
never listened
to 'Blue Mink'.
They didn't know
that what we
needed was
a great big melting pot.
My parents did –
they had me

The 'Ugandan Asian' crisis hit
and I became called
a 'Paki' overnight
because Enoch was right
and I should go back
to where I came from
even though
I was 'there' already

and to some Asian kids
I was a 'gori'

and the white girls
didn't stay too long
because they
didn't want to be
called "dogmeat!"
by their peers
and parents.
Shove thy neighbour
So tell me -
what the hell
is the colour of love?

And the 'Rastas'
wore Wales football tops-
they were red
gold and green.
To them I was
a threat also –
'Babylon!'

I could not
go back to Africa;
a place I'd
never been
And my heroes
all spoke perfect English -
Sidney Poitier, CLR James

The old-old ladies
in Cardiff's docks

told me about
the real Africans –
when they came,
how tall they were,
how smart they were
in top hats, spats and canes...

And my grandad
was a 'Cru' man
and then he
joined a crew.
He sailed
the seven seas
and settled in
the Bay of Tigers –
raised a family.

And my father was a 'half caste' –
that's what they
said back then.
And he would
sing Calypso
as he did the washing up –
but said
Jamaicans were
johnny-come-lately's.

As I got older
boundaries blurred
Bigotry, which
came in waves,
rescinded
like the tide

I became
'exotic' –
Amerindian?
Latin-American?
Because of long
straight black hair
and melanin-
darkened skin –
myth-maken identity
yet again

And I don't know
where I come from –
but you don't know
where I'm going.
But I do worry
that the tide is
coming in again
and
sometimes I
(really do)
'feel like
throwing my hands
up in the air'
so – goodbye butterfly,
you have spread
your wings.
And I
have been stung
by the world…

Menna Elfyn

Four Poems

SWALLOW

Birds we understand,
spend crumbs in garden,
at back door's eye:
understand their need
to break bread with us.

And are we not birds who
don't always flock together?
The sky a high refuge,
Lonely, knowing we'll land, meet
beak's needs, at heartbreaks.

And in every firmament
migrators mingle, mixing
heaven and earth for shelter,
wayfarers a-wing,
seeking a new nest,
a fair resting place.

So those birds, warm-feathered,
should remember the withouters
scouring the soil
in search of common grounds.

One smile a spring,
one swallow making summer.

COUPLINGS

Life is a house in ruins. And we mean to fix it up
and make it snug. With our hands we knock it into
    shape
to the very top. Till beneath this we fasten a roofbeam
that will watch the coming and going of our skyless life
two crooked segments. They are fitted together
timbers in concord. Smooth beams, and wide.
Two in touch. That's the craft we nurture in folding
doubled flesh on a frame. Conjoining the smooth cou-
    plings
that sometimes arch into one. Aslant above a cold
    world,
hollow wood wafting passion. Then stock still for a
    time.
And how clear-cut the roof, creaking love at times,
as it chides the worm to keep off and await its turn.

Translated from the Welsh by Joseph P. Clancy

ILLUMINATION

Oh, how I love this message,
and the anonymous ambassador
who demands my promise:

that, on leaving, I shall
extinguish the ever-friendly light,

become a mediator
between those who came,

those who left
and those still to come.

A scribbled note between the one and the other
to say we fully understand darkness

and light; understand its certainty,
this thing the world rolled out of,

as we step into space
turning the cold into a furnace

with a fingertip, seeing a small lamp
blossom, an universe under the promising moon,

and then, as suddenly as a pupil dilating,
stepping out of the room

holding on to the chain of words
as I extinguish the light

until the place, in the blink of an eye,
grows dark

and I am disillusioned. And maybe this

is how light first came into the word –
God tired of blindness and shouted

'Light,' and there was light

— but forgot one tiny detail:
the selfishness of man.

And this is why I love
the new, loving messenger

who chastises me gently with the words:
'Will the last person to leave the room
please switch off the light?'

Sometimes I almost feel
like leaving a message myself,

writing – "Lest God in black space
should one day shout 'Let there be darkness'."

And there will be darkness.

STONES

The doorstep of your being
is every morning's clean slate.

The capstone of my soul,
just one step and I set it
firm and true in the wall of love.

I never understood
the hunger for crystals, a nugget of gold,
a diamond. Just gave thanks

for the stones in my hand—
sometimes a thunderbolt straight from the sky,
a lodestone, two ships in harbour,

a magnet to draw the senses,
a menhir in an age of gravel:
it moves, without gathering moss.

The whetstone of my mind,
two flints striking a firestorm
to rage in the quarry of flesh that we mine.

Stone on stone, the milestones
I walk to gladly,
the spark in my heart like two stones singing.

Translated from the Welsh by Joseph P. Clancy

CERDD GAREGOG

Carreg ddrws dy fodolaeth,
sy'n llechen lân y bore.

Maen ar gronglwyd f'enaid,
un cam wrth fur cariad
sy raid. Un syml, sownd.

Wnes i ddim deall helfa
pobl am risial, neu glap aur,
na deimwnt. Dim ond

diolch am y meini mewn llaw,
meini mellt weithiau o'r awyr,
maen sugn, dwy long mewn harbwr,

maen tynu atat synnwyr
a'r maen hir mewn oes o raean
fe dreigla heb fwsogli.

Maen hogi fy ymennydd,
meini cellt, yn mynnu tanchwa
dan feinwe'n chwarel grai.

Maen ar faen yn gerrig milltir
y cerddaf atynt yn llawen,
gan delori fel clap y cerrig.

Jon Gower

Joybirds

For Eric

Swifts, birds of summer
Startle Welsh sky on scythe-shaped wings,
Their sooty brown plumes all bakelite black at this
distance

Harvesting high, wildly aloft above the rooftops,
They are celebrations of such days,
Uncorking velocity
    Windriding,
      Winnowing spaces so wide they
are not spaces
On curved wings
That cut the plastic air.

At dusk they scimitar
Hithering, turning and thithering

Their electric shrieks
Like miniaturised banshees.

Little wonder then that they were called
Devil birds, as they trawled their open gapes
Like trawl nets through seas of midges,
A pollen of gnats, a dusting of damselfly vol-ou-vents.

They have other names here
Gwrach yr ellyll, goblin's witch
Asgell hir, long wing

Aderyn yr eglwys, the church bird
Aderyn du'r llan, the black bird of the bank
Y biwita
Y folwen, whitebelly,
Marthen du, black martin,
Y wennol ddu fawr, the great black swallow,
Biwits
Gwennol gwblddu, the all black swallow
Gwennol fuan, the early swallow

A veritable litany of them.

Then, you'd expect so many…
A bird that lives in such proximity,
Under eaves, nesting
Over towns, trawling

And then in winter, other skies

Over the Sanaga river
In Cameroon they join others…
Little swifts and African palms
African black and Bates's
An aerial cavalcade of species
Bulleting over reeds

And rising higher now, arcing above the rainforests
Which swell and billow with a thousand greens –
Emerald, Irish moss, Hooker's green,
The greenleaf of mahogany, ebony, obeche,
Dibetu, sapelli, boubinga, zebra wood,
More greens than we can countenance.

There they are, the startle-birds,

Needling the skies of the Congo basin
Darning together the seasons
Making of summer and winter one great mantle,

Making their home, however temporary

Where the light is.

Aliya Kabba

Three Poems

WHERE ARE YOU FROM?

Where are you from?
Cardiff, Manchester, London
I'm Bajan, Grenadian
Awarwak, I'm Indian
Nationality, ethnicity, identity
Where are you?
Where do you belong?

The answer I reply is never sufficient
But who are you?
Why can you tell me that I am deficient?
Is it cause I'm black?
No joke, is it because I am black?

Does that make you uncomfortable?
When you were the one to ask
Why are you black and in Britain?
And now you're left with the task
Of removing the forbidden curtain

I say curtain as I'm trying to be polite
But I see it in plain sight
And I suppose that's the British in me
But it's time that you see
When you don't accept who I say I am
And you continue to plea
You draw the curtain

So you're there and here's me

Maybe I'm not being clear
Let me spell it out so you can really hear
If you don't accept who I say I am
Because I am black
That is racism
No, this is not an attack
It's not a criticism
Its fact

That was an awkward conversation
But one I've had over and again
And it never eases, that sensation
Of anger, loss and pain
As we had a good connection
But they couldn't hear what I was saying

How can they be racist?
They have black friends
How can they be racist?
Should I let them make amends
Because they stand with me?
They show their solidarity
Power to the people
One nation
You hear them say
We're all God's creation
So why can't they see my identity from within?
Outside, I identify by the colour of my skin

FIGHTING

I'm tired
Of fighting
I've been fighting for so long
In this ring
He punched me and I hit the ropes
But I bounce back
Ready to fight again
Some have knocked me to the floor
But I pull myself up to stand
Ready to fight again
But I'm tired of fighting
Sometimes I raise my hands up
I protect myself
I know what's coming
But he dances around me
Such a pretty dance
I eventually drop my guard
As soon as he lands a punch
I'm on the floor again
This time the ref starts counting
I want to stay here
On the floor
But I have no choice
I have to get up to fight again
I'm tired of fighting
I've been in this ring for forty rounds
Maybe more
But each punch is just as painful as the last
I'm waiting for the day I hear the bell

And for the ref to enter the ring
Grab me by the wrist
Raising up my arm
To announce that I am the winner
And he
This one
Will sweep me off my feet
Raise me up onto his shoulders
And carry my broken bleeding battered and bruised
heart
Out of the ring
The fight is over
He holds my heart so delicately
Knowing all the fights it's been through
I'm tired of fighting
And the fight is finally over

NAKED IN THE STREET

Naked in the street
How dare they, how dare he
Strip me
Of what is mine because of me
Because of what he sees

What is it about me?
My dress is below the knee
What did I do?
I shouldn't have worn these heeled shoes
I'm now naked in the street

Is it my apple bottom,
Peach breasts or cherry lips?
Is it my sloping shoulders,
Wide eyes or the way I swing my hips?

This fruit market is closed
But even if she wore more clothes
Then by the time she passed him
He would strip her including her grin

So we're naked in the street
Clothed women stripped bare
Naked in the street, naked

But we're only
Apples, peaches and cherries
He's only interested in the flesh
He can't handle our cores
Don't let him touch it
For he will never think

What about what we think
What we feel
What we know
What about the lives we touch
And the seeds we sow
Why can't he see that our cores?
Have the seeds to help us grow?

He will never see you or me
But leave us naked in the street
With all eyes on us
And no one to trust

Next time
Wear more clothes

Suryatapa Mukherjee

Three Poems

HOW TO SPELL MY NAME

This was a dream –
United Kingdom!
Europeans!
Christmas!
And modernity.

Freedom.

This wasn't just my dream,
It was our dream;
Us in countries less fortunate
After years of losing to this place.
Well, centuries
Of looting
And killing.
We are left a little scarred.
And this place,
We saw, as our paradise.

The land of promise!
It doesn't matter which country,
As long as it is 'the West'
That we see on TV,
And the radio,
On the paper,
And in our books.
A palace of dreams.

I used to love this place
Before visiting it.
We used to love this place
Before visiting it.

Now, we hate it
And it's not just the weather.
Now, we hate it
Like prisoners on an island
Built on false hopes.

But if we make it,
Ah, there is security.

The mirror cracks when you know
That detention centres have higher walls
Than prisons.

Detention centres have barbed wires
Pricklier for people of colour arriving,
Than prisons for British criminals.

Two months in a place like that
And a teacher forgot how to read.

Two months in a place like that
And a teacher forgot how to read?

In this promised land,
People of promise
Fade,
Decay,
Disappear
In wait, for years.

People of promise,
People with potential –
Intelligent,
Ambitious,
Full of talent.
Fade, decay, disappear.

All my friends have left.
Some others would too if they could.

You see, it's not easy.
We're not just let in through an open gate
And handed a life of dreams.

I once met a Syrian refugee,
An engineer,
Who can now never be an engineer,
Never have that career,
Because he is a refugee
In the UK.

English is a foreigner on his tongue.
He wants to wed a Syrian girl.
But now, he can never leave.
You see, he is wasting away
And he knows it.

Immigrants have their dreams
Peeled from their skin
Too often.

But I know why you're suspicious and inhospitable.
Because you are terrible guests.

The Kohinoor, in your museum

And your crown,
Was taken 'legally'
From a boy of ten
While his mother, the queen,
Was in prison.

Churchill starved us.
Yes.
And millions of me died.
Twice.
Churchill killed millions of me
And he wasn't alone,
And he wasn't the first.
Do we call it famine,
Or the white man's priority?

For our first big mutiny,
We were punished heavily.
And Charles Dickens said,
If it was up to him,
He would exterminate my race, completely.

Once a man massacred thousands of me in Punjab.
We never forget!
Once a man massacred thousands of us in Punjab.
Enclosed space.
No escape.
Not a bullet wasted, he said.
Then the people in Great Britain,
The people here, themselves,
Raised 26000 pounds
As a reward for his duty.

The white man's duty

Is leading a massacre
To keep what was never his.

We have been here, in this place,
For longer than you care to remember.
We have always been here.

We fought in your world wars.
Yes, both wars.
We were promised our freedom
In exchange for yours.
We kept our end of the bargain,
And you? Well.

London was diverse from the start.
The Roman Empire
Had people from all over the world
In positions of power and less.

If you look at the royal family
With a magnifying lens,
You'll find black ancestry
In more than Meghan Markle.

You don't know all of that.
If they taught you all of that,
You'd know how to say my name.

You'd know, I built this country
As much as you;
I have been here as long as you.
You'd see me.
And you'd see yourself.

And you'd know *how* to spell my name.

I HAVE A COMPLICATED RELATIONSHIP WITH MY FATHER

When people say good and evil
Do not live separately,
I know it is true,
For I have lived with my father.

He grew up with a strange sort of evil
Which is unleashed at home;
And outside, its face is charity.

I love my father
And he loves me too.
But we have crossed arms in battle
More than once.
And the battlegrounds were his ego,
And my ego,
And the claim for the more stubborn,
And the title of the more righteous.

My father worshipped his father,
And he grew into him.
And they both housed good and evil
In their every whim.

You see, their evil
Came out to bite others
Into blood and broken skin.

But when it comes to his kids,
My father is a feminist.
And yet, we have crossed arms in battle
More than once.

I see political incorrectness
When he says he raised his daughters like sons.
But he uses his privilege
To give my voice an audience.

I remember filling out a form
For a pan card or some.
And it said to provide a parent's name.
My defiant pen, of course,
Wrote down my mother's.
My father threw a tantrum.
You see, in my country,
You only use your mother's name
If your father is dead.

In his cultural context,
He saw it as my biggest slight to him.
Like I was knifing at some cord
That ties our kin.

I held up my head
With my nose in the air.
I have a mother who is equal to my father.
And I'll have the government acknowledge her.

So, we went to the office.
And the woman there,
Collecting the form,
Said that it is wrong.
My father raised his head
And said, 'It's okay. Let her.'

So, you see,

I have a complicated relationship with my father.

This one time I took all his demons
And laid them in front of him.
In life-like likeness,
They screamed in ink.
He went and sat at the nearest temple
For two days.
Not a word, escaped his lips.

My mother did too,
On our terrace a while back.
We sat on the carpet
In the cool evening breeze.
Like always,
She told the tales of horror -
Of when she came to her husband's place.
After all was done and said once again,
My father said he would marry us
To a man different from him.

You see my father is running from his demons.
And sometimes I forget -
That the birds of my thought
Wouldn't be flying to point B,
If my father's dreams
Hadn't flown to point A.

This one time, I had written
How he had saved me from drowning
When I was aged ten.
Well, I made it a little tale
Of gratitude.

But come his birthday,
We had another fight
And he didn't receive it.

When he was building his new warehouse
He told me to design it on paper
I told him the trees must not be cut
My mother dismissed it
The roots would break the concrete
It was an impossible idea

To this day
If you visit it
You will see great big green trees
Rising from between the bricks
They built the warehouse
Around them

An unthinkable idea
Thought up by an impossible teen
But my father made it happen
Because I asked for it

You see, even though
I am stuck in a rut
Of immigration
And paperwork;
And finding a job
Is a citizen's dream,
My father said
I'm writing poetry at least.

But I write in English

And he only speaks his
Mother's Bengali.
Someday, I want to master his tongue,
So, I can write in his language.
And show him the colours of my dreams,
And the birds of my mind,
Oh, how wildly they fly!

For now, I only tell him stories
Of my stories
And my poems.
And oh, the things I have done!
Sometimes they fly outside his mind's reach.

But one day, he'll see them.
And I tell him, people will know him
Because of me.
He doesn't question it
He only teases it won't happen in his lifetime
But I know he is proud already.

CLOSETS

Panic!
Quick!
Bring the vacuum,
The dettol,
The gloves.
Clean out the bowels
Of the wood,
The strands of the cloth.
Soak it hot and wet.
Disinfect.

Can you smell it:
The lack of love,
The emptying of affection?
Smell the amnesia.
Smell 'platonic'.

Quick!
Hide the sex.
Hide the anxiety.
Hide history.

Is it blank enough?
Quick!
What do I call you?
Friend?
Or nothing?
Only pronoun.
Which pronoun?
Quick!
Can you tell my nails mean bite?

Can you tell my nails mean love?
Blink twice.
Pout 'I love you'.
Can you tell how many years?
Does it feel like zero? Good.

Quick!
Throw my hand away.
Quick!
Change subject.

Don't say 'visa'.
Don't say 'illegal'.
Don't say 'colonial'.
Don't say 'I'm trying to live here
Because you made it illegal there.'

Don't say 'Don't.'

Don't say 'freedom' and 'future'.
Don't say 'us'.
Don't tell them.

Honk!
It's okay,
I'm not human,
It's okay!
Honk.

Cover
Under.
Touch.
Memorise.
Miss in anticipation.

Picture separation.

Imagine the sleeping body
Being wheeled away.
Watch lips fall into mouth,
Eyes empty,
Skin melting.

Watch pictures fade,
Time fall.

Stop.
Memorise.
Hold.

Happy anniversary.

Kange Ernest

Two Poems

TO MY MENTOR, R.I.P BATE BISONG

First Day at school.
A million miles from home
Waiting for the bell to go
Why are they all big, other children?
So noisy? So much at home, they must
Have been born in uniform, live all
Their lives in playgrounds, spent years inventing
Games that are rough, that swallow you up.
And the railings, all around, the railings
Are they there to keep out wolves and
Monsters?
Things that carry off and eat children?
Things you do not take sweet from.
Perhaps they are to stop us getting out running
 away from lesson, lesson.
What does lesson looks like?
Sound small and strong
They keep them in the glass
rooms. Room made of glass
Imagine!
I wish I could remember my name
Mummy said it will come in useful
Like wellies when there is puddles
Yellow wellies. I wish she was here
I think my name is sown on somewhere

Perhaps the teacher will read it for me.
Teacher, the one who makes the tea for me.
The academic tea.

THE VERY SLAVES OF TOLE

The very neo-colonial slaves.
Everyone abandoned you.
They did not harken to
Your plight, they became
Deft and dumb, mute, blind in the
Very bright of their eyes.
They're heartless
But you're priceless.
They murdered their
Own in the light of
An indifferent globe.

They stole your blood,
Your sweat, your hope, your 'ngum',
The future of your offspring.
You begged knees scraped
For what is yours.
You slept on wood, hardened beds
Grassy Bed mercy on you.

You became night-watches
On the corridors of

Those who stole from
And sucked you dry.
But the mosquitoes
On you had mercy.
And gave you a comfortable
Night.
You abandoned your
Children for a great trek
With tattered clothes and
No foot pads to beg for,
Your Own milk from your
Pirates, your thieves, your robbers.
Some were mercy snatched freed
By death, frustration, hopelessness
On the course to get their blood
And sweat worth.
Some maimed for life, some became blind
Never will they see
Their expecting love ones again left
Behind.

Cruelty!
Some were tugged to
Earth without a grave,
No befitting caskets,
No shawl, no funeral
No ones to mourn.

Some nursing mums
Lost their children
Cos hunger dried up

Infested breasts could
No longer a drop worth.

Oh! What a world!
Evasramote, where were you

Feed you did we not

poor Nguenguerous

Gods,
Are you still sleeping?
Wake up! and see your
Children lying down
Like mourners waiting
For a missing corps
Like trashes in a trash-can.
They were patriots
They were heroes
Dehumanized.
They say
You are worthless
You are hopeless.
But your children say
You are worthful
You are hopeful
But not homeless
Dry your tears
For I have seen
A William Wilberforce.

Kale Dante

Six Poems

FATHOMLESS SEA

Hollowed, cold, an empty vessel at the bottom of the
fathomless sea that is my heart,
I grit my teeth with the last energy my weak body can
        muster,
a grieving surge of abnormal electric wave, forces my
        heart to deflate
Soon, it shall contort to resemble the monster that faces
        me.

If in your wildest dream, you stood face to face with it,
if in Dante's peak, you see what I saw,
you lose your tang of every fine object.

Those images play in my mind a bad tango,
they come and go with every slumber, if I puke,
I am left without intestines of the same size,
having shrink for lack of sustenance,
'Its food not poison when taste buds die'
What did you tell them?

They butchered my kin, it was child's play.
In my sleep, I lay awake
tortured by endless voices
of pain and longing for life cut short
When those bullets rained,
a bloodied path like it was Passchendaele
though this was no war

the sad songs as they died,
shrills of pain in my ears
Gathered like a swamp of bee songs in a plantation,
'these were my kin'
their voices in unison, saying
'Go tell them, we didn't journey for free'
I saw a youngster, bowels hanging out from a bullet-hole,
I saw heads riddled with holes,
blood flowing into an everlasting sea
Eyes, looking at horizons beyond.
That moment, we spoke silently,
as if I should understand his dying wish,
was it that old lie?
That his blood was a seed of liberty
like those of martyrs long gone?
Those eyes bade me farewell,
I am an emissary,
on this pillow I lay awake,
sleep has left my eyes,
the shrine scattered into pieces,
I have my ears on the ground,
terror reigns
'Mourners bring flowers, grave diggers dig'
the villagers are out in numbers,
widows and widowers
sweeping the bullets in reverse.

MY FIRST WHITE HAIR

To my first white hair for a birthday, thank you all.
It shot up alone amongst the thick forest of my black
      beard,
At first shy and hidden in the thick mass of difference,
Unnoticed by eyes different from mine,
I marveled at her grace to stand alone,
Delicately I groom her
Wooing her to stand out from the crowd.

A Herculean task it seems then,
Day after day she struggled out to stand out,
And I struggled to understand the time past,
From childhood to a man,
What had gone wrong and what was good and sweet,
I had anticipated her coming, but not so soon
I had envied her from afar
So too will I, outgrown her attention like a child to a
      new toy,

My first white hair, she won't be the first
As my winter comes slowly but surely
She will be joined by others to outshine the blacks,
Then I shall be called an old man,
I shall look back with fondness of a time of spring
And say ,I too was once young with no white hair.
Adieu to the blacks and welcome to the whites of hairs.

LOST IN PAIN

If only you could stay even for a moment,
So I could touch you and yell how much I love you,
If only you stayed and teach me, teach me the ways of
      our kin,
That sacred paths of old
So in turn I may teach your line,
If only you could stay, I wouldn't worry as do I
Of my own aegis,

Am some cowering man transformed,
If only you could stay oh! My winsome yet a fierce
king
And not take away my vim in your exit
How now I wish for that 'prelapsarian' fondness of
      childhood,

I need you and not want you,
Blood runs no more in my veins
Memories flood her routes
Not your exit that banishes me to these extremes,

But firm reality of never to behold you no more,
Such shame
Did I make you proud
Did I get under your skin?

Did you see me in you
Answer await me beyond
Papa I miss you then and now
Lost in these conflagrations of pain.

MY GROWING

My papa was tall,
father to him was tall,
among men they stood tall,
Their fame never did rest in any hall.

What we have, they lacked,
What they had we lacked,
Where then is our knack,
Or shall we all be jacked?

When shall we do our growing
For the cock has been crowing
Or then, there shall be no crowning
No I will not be frowning
I shall be growing.

FREEDOM CALLS

The call has been made
Not a call of words spoken by orators
Not one from scribbled manifestos
Nor from dictates,
The call comes from the drums of old
Made from the baobab
With a mix from the 'matanda'
Preserved from birth
The sound is of freedom
Carried not by the town criers
But spread by the violent winds of change
From runnels to the sea
It softly caresses our senses
And surely wins our hearts
From old to young
Weak and strong
We are summoned
Where we go from here is of our making
We mar, or we make it to the sands of time
Our names forever in history tales
Our shame and pride, a line drawn
We answer to the drums of wisdom
Lest we wallow in the backyard of slavery
Whilst we tell our children that old lie
Of "we did our best"
Heed to the drums of old
It never fooled our past
They won against the enslavers
Ask the Germans of Kuva

There's a tale of broomstick
It's no far-fetched myth
There's a song to inspire
And a pain to motivate
Freedom calls to be answered
The drums beat louder
The message stronger
Yet we still contemplate at meetings of egos
While charlatans dance deceit
Then it's a sound only for the brave
It's a call to a dance of strength
And not for weaklings
They who hear have heard
And speak those who talk
At the end freedoms calls us all homeward

STORIES OF MY PEOPLE

Gathered around the chimney
The fire lit and glowing
With everything to roast
Children of my father
We listened with attention
From our father
The stories of our ancestors
Ngoe and Sumediang
Their love and pain
Their exploits as they moved
Their children as they found tribes
And where we got our pride
From generations to generations
These stories pass down
From father to sons
To be with us forever
My favorite, was the white hunter
In the forbidden forest of our clan
How he was fooled by our gods
Chased out never to return
Where shall I gather my children
To pass these stories down
For the television has taken over
And the fire now a gas cooker

Gareth Writer-Davies

Three Poems

BREATHE

my mother lies
in a hospital in Cape Town

she is weak
and the doctor has yet to decide
what to do

she was found on the beach
confused
short of breath

they have found tangles in her brain
and there will be changes
and I must be strong

my mother lies
in a hospital in Cape Town
tells everyone that the country's gone to the dogs
since the blacks took over

when I rang
she asked if she was going mad

I did not tell her
she was sedated
with an anti-psychotic drug

so we talked about the rain

in this waiting game of telephone calls
the truth
is only the first casualty

my mother lies
in a hospital in Cape Town
her breathing though shallow now regular

and I am grateful
and shall not give in
to her small destructions of character

I know
that as she breathes
so do I

and tomorrow
I must fly
to bring her home again

PELARGONIUM

a scarlet geranium
(that is what your grandmother called it)
flowers
at twenty degrees

soaking up the sun
the leaves and the calyx of the bud
are fuzzy
which makes the pelargonium difficult to love

naked (like nature intended)
you
wait for the perfect tan

I fade my eyes
think about the cultivation of species
and Babylon

JAWCH

people no longer believe in the devil
nor good and evil

which is fine (and dandy)
but
we now take good as the natural outcome

of actions
that would have seen us hung in less tolerant ages

evil
is only for shady neighbours and shadier politicians

when we take a chance and look in the mirror
do we suspect

that the Age of Reason
was really one big lesson in introspection?

and what lies beneath tautology
is our own reflection?

Dylan Moore

Five Poems

I. DARK MIRROR

I am Welsh.

You can hear it in
the way I say
school and bowl and owl, with
two generous sing-song syllables
like my mother.

You can research it.

Look up my bilingual birth
certificate: Casnewydd/Newport,
evidence to file
alongside my forebears
in Portmanmoor Road and Porth

and yet and yet and yet

when I was born, the doctor asked about
my mother's origins.

My father (being
white) remained invisible:
his mudcrawling
famine-avoiding
potato-munching
immigrant ancestors had long since left
the workhouse.

Being foreign herself, the doctor
was not attuned
to my mother's lilt
as local as the bricks and trees.
Instead she saw
in my mongolian spot,
a circular bruise in the small of my back,
a dark mirror, an alternative
umbilicus. Difference.

Reciting three, four, more
generations
was not enough.
'Which island?' she demanded,
learning that my mother's mother
was from St Kitts, and not having heard of it
on her form she wrote 'Jamaica'
– a fine country
where no one in my family has ever been.

II. DEOXYRIBONUCLEIC DENDROCHRONOLOGY

My family tree must be
a conifer, shaped as it is
like a triangle:
my mother and father and me.

Its point points pastwards
from Great Britain
to the Caribbean,
and back to Africa.

A single swab
of saliva reveals all,
a tea-leaf telling in reverse:
black bodies patterned like pilchards.

The test recognises the ghosts
of my ancestors
in Mali and Ghana and Congo
and Cameroon

taken and stripped
of names

but the double helix
of nucleotides
inside me is as sure
as the rings of a tree

I am West African.

III. MUSEUM OF WELSH LIFE

There is a row of stone cottages
at the open-air museum
where you can travel through time.

Each door opens onto a scene
prepared carefully to imply
residents momentarily popped out:

early eighties, a radio is on
and china collectibles evoke a royal wedding,
the beginning of that long, slow tragedy;

nineteenth century life denoted
by the simple flickering of flame,
embers long since cold burn again

and on the mantelpiece, a framed,
embroidered bible verse declares:
As for me and my house,
we will serve the Lord.

IV. (NEVER) STILL LIFE, BUEA

Cockerels and Afropop,
an alternative dawn
chorus, soundtrack the

every third day water
collection – bright
plastic buckets swing in the sun.

Tinny sound systems sing
chop my money chop my money
cos I don't care, I don't care.

Outside my mosquito net
and beyond the window
flies swarm drying fish

and buckled-axle taxis,
five to the backseat,
declare Jesus is Lord.

Someone, it seems
is talking to me.

V. DAMASCUS IN A MINIBUS

I wrestled with St Paul
on the minibus from Limbe,
after the gunboats
and mangrove swamp
pirate-waters of Bakassi.

We met at Mermoz
and danced at Chariots,
found love among the
indomitable lions replica
shirts in the market at Douala.

I found life on the streets
of Buea, and God found me –
running, in the end –
to a tin and concrete hut
on the outskirts of Small Soppo.

Bethany Rivers

Five Poems

POSTED ON THE QUIET

Finally, last night, I did it.
Although I'm now sitting
in a cell in this stinking jail

of sweat and fear, I'm grinning.
I stole in to the private rooms
in Westminster and I graffitied

on every wall and every mirror
the names of all the benefit suicides.
I prit-sticked photos to MPs' desks,

sellotaped them on plush seated chairs.
I then confettied the Speaking House
with photos of Aunt Beryl (put her head

in the oven), odd-job-man-Billy always
ready with a smile (took an overdose)
young Sally (mother of twins) hung herself,

stuck them down with chewing gum
along the central aisle,
all the way to the Speaker's chair.

AT SEVENTEEN

The mirror shows a blurred reflection
in the ladies' toilet of the Faversham.

The usual crowd drinking
shandies, coke and half pints
in our college lunch hour.

The pool table draws us again.
The addiction of not potting balls enthrals.

I came in here to cry.
You follow me in.
Tell me I'm over reacting. The knife drives
in a little deeper. Of all people –
I expected you to understand

The boy taking the next shot
at his final red
does not know my world has
cracked seismically
because of him.

I dream of my body
under the tyres of a lorry.
But you told me
I was over reacting.

He pots the red
into the black hole.
Tomorrow will be
another day, another girl.

HIRAETH

There is longing, my friend, and there is longing.
– Zeina Hashem Beck

Home is not where you think it is, nor is it where
you remember: it's not bricks & mortar
or the place where your parents reside;
some say home is a memory you keep
locked in your heart, but you continuously lose
the key; some say home is the time before
you were born & the time after you die; some say
home is the body you perspire in; some say home
is the hara, the seat of the soul. Love songs declare
home is in the eyes of your lover, or the resonance
of his voice. But I say Home is in the act
of writing. Home is a recitation of Persian poetry,
though you don't understand a word. Home is
in the eyes of a golden statue of Buddha
in a foreign land. Home is in the smell of garlic
on your fingers, three days after you cooked
the curry. Home is a song you keep on losing,
keep hoping to remember.

NO VOICE

(After Rebecca Perry / Zeina Hashem Beck / Seni Seneviratne)

I, with no voice under an aching blue sky, devoid
of the lift of honey, flights of bees, Easter Sunday,
violets. My mythology is crazed in pavings of
empty chocolate eggs. I crave fire. Flame
the glass of night. It belongs to the phoenix.

Fill the glass with broken dreams. Have
it over ice with a blood red straw broken
with hopes that were never described. I see through
the mirror my own invisibility: the silk veil reflecting
broken sunshine, caught on the rocks.

Night is the only true drink and I drink it down
greedily & too soon for too long. Don't.
It won't heal you like that. I know
like the moon knows its orbit
how black the early hours of the mind are.

I tongued the engraving of your name. You stole the food
of my mind. The energy and strength of it. The egg of it.
But dark is a thing that learns how to grow from within. I'm
that close to being defeated by my own words. Bottle happy

lingers on my tongue, makes fools of us all
for on that very day, the voices of the dead flare. Listen.
My breath in the wings of a butterfly, lips that thirst
& crack & wait for gentle things.

TIME IS SOFTER

you don't have to race the poison
or sweet-tongue the nectar

it is not life or death every second
it is not heaven or hell every second

there's a quiet between each tick
which softly expands with every in-breath

and it's in this timeless quiet of expansion
between the strings of harps and guitars

between the drum beats of Africa
and the salsa steps of Spain

there's a softness you remember
of mother-hush, a deepening lullaby shush

in the dreams carried by feather-breath songs
in the petals of unfurling roses

the indent your head leaves on your pillow
and rises again, like the sun

Mike Jenkins

Six Poems

ARWRES

I Marie

Y ferch hon yw cyffredin ac arbennig,
Curiad y teulu, llaw a cheg.

Y ferch sy'n gyrru'r tacsi bob dydd,
Helpu pan o't ti'n cwympo ar y stryd.

Y ferch sy'n wrando ar bob gair,
Hwyr y nos a chynnar y bore.

Y ferch sy'n dy gefnogi di yn y cae
Pan nad wyt ti'n gallu chwarae.

Y ferch sy'n nyrs, cogydd ac athrawes,
Dy hen ffrind, gofalwraig mor gynnes.

Y ferch sy'n caru heb gwestiwn
Drwy'r tymor peryglus llais ar y ffon.

Fel anrhegion, wedi rhoi ei hamser a'i phres,
Siwr y fod, mae hi'n arwres.

HEROINE

To Marie

This woman's ordinary and special,
rhythm of the family, hand and mouth.

A taxi-driver every single day,
helped you up whenever you fell.

A woman who listens to every word
late at night or early in the morning.

A woman supporting when you play,
even if things go awry.

A woman who is nurse, cook and teacher,
an old friend, a warm carer.

A woman who loves without question
through tough times, a voice on the phone.

Giving gifts of her money and time,
she is indeed a heroine.

Translated by the author.

IF I WOZ A BUILDIN

If I become a buildin
they'd afto do summin.

I'd ave a grant,
they'd do me up tidee.

I'd feel clean f once,
with new materials coverin.

People from all over
ud come an visit me,

take loadsa selfies,
I'd even be on-a telly.

Istree an eritage, look at im,
shows ow the town's improvin!

If I woz a buildin
instead of a young marn

searchin f the next igh,
wanderin without ope,

they'd give me a fancy name,
ewse me f advertisin.

Now I see theyer looks condemn
as they mutter 'Scum!'

I COME YER

I come yer   all-a way from ower valley
excapin to the city,
fire-fightin in-a famlee

I come yer   tha voice still strong
inside o me,
my missis a Cockney

I come yer   never thought I'd see,
never thought I'd be there
in such a rich Boro

I come yer   an woz like my ol man
tellin me stories of Aberfan –
pullin out children, joy an d'pression

I come yer   though now I wonder
ave we really got further ?
It's the same ol ladder

I come yer   an jest like my father
them memrees 're nightmares,
loud sounds t soldiers

I come yer –   the pooer under a tip
the pooer trapped in a Tower,
justice be'ind barriers o paper.

ATTIC MUSIC

The bird that was trapped in the attic,
one we neither saw nor heard
could have dislodged them.

All I know is, they fell and floated
down from the square opening,
white feathers in dots and lines.

We caught and collected them :
Debussy, Elgar, Saint-Saens ,
annotated for your fingering.

Each one a testament to hours
of practice ; the mirror on the landing
where you sought perfection.

The plastic bag had been tattered,
the music within musty but intact.
The bird had died or escaped.

So we put them back together
by that long, slim mirror,
feather upon feather, compiling.

One day you'll take them away
and they will fly from your bow
over the moor into the sky.

LONDON PARAKEETS

I look up
at the squawking birds
in the tall tree
near my son's flat
expecting crows or rooks,
only to be astonished
by rose-ringed parakeets
like escapees from an aviary
or some airport crate,
or a film studio

in just one street
the odours mingle
from all over the world :
hot breaths of chilli,
burnt edges of pizza,
spices of cumin and coriander
in the brown misty air

the continents come
to settle here
in parks and avenues, the familiar ;
these startling foreign birds
now everyday inhabitants ,
their bright exotic green
tangs on the tongue's tip.

Ndumbe Lyonga La Manjinja

Nene

Nene feared the frightful looks on Maty's face. As soon as they were pronounced husband and wife, Nene knew she was damned. Until that time Maty was Mr. Nice Guy. After the marriage ceremony, once Maty had delivered two pigs to Nene's family, she effectively became his slave. Nene fetched water from the fast rivers on the foot of the mountain, she looked after the tomato plants, she even took a job working part time at the tea plantation. None of this seemed to please Maty who would always look for reasons to raise his hands at Nene, beating her black and blue. At nights the neighbours will hear Nene cry, but no one dared to challenge Maty. Maty's meal was either too hot or too cold, and this will be followed by punches raining down on Nene's face. He will grab Nene by the ears, pull her head and at times make her sleep on the small 'ewongo' where she shared the space with three goats.

After Nene gave birth to their first child, the violence only increased. 'That child doesn't even resemble me – I see how you always talk to Monyama the village wrestler, the baby looks like him, did you sleep with Monyama?' Even before Nene could say No and plead her defence, slaps upon slaps would fall on her face.

One morning Maty complained of severe stomach ache, afraid he had been poisoned by Nene, he summoned the gods. The gods advised him to take what we call 'wezrongi' enema using grass called 'masrepu'. Maty shouted out for Nene to take the baby and go fetch him some fresh water from the stream on the foot of the mountain.

This was her moment, Nene decided to escape here horrors. Baby on her back, calabash oh her head, she left the house and headed toward the direction of the stream, she took a detour and headed towards the house of her uncle who lived not far away in the neighbouring village.

'Who goes there?' uncle Njila roared from the veranda. 'People fear me, what brings you here?'

'I am running away from my husband. Over the past two years, there has never been a day that goes by without him beating me'

'Is your husband mad? Who is he that chases a woman and a two months old baby? I wish I could help but I have my own problems, someone stole six of my pigs last night. Sorry I cannot help you'

'Please uncle Njila, I am begging you to help me'

'Go away, I do not wish to invite trouble into my house. Go away'

Nene left the house, following the stars she took into the bushes, she followed a familiar path, the grounds, the bushes where she uses to play with her twin brother. She came across a gathering of village elders, they listened to her story again they refused to help her. They had heard rumours of the strength of Maty and they did not want to invite trouble into their homes. They fed Nene and the child and bid her fare well and good luck. She cried but her tears were not visible – –

Nene followed the path until she came to a small village. Her twin brother Tua was a village elder.

As Nene narrated her ordeal, Tua cried: 'Why did you suffer alone? Why didn't you call for me? I am going to kill Maty, I will kill him I promise you'.

Tua, anticipating the coming of Maty in search of his estranged wife, decided to dig a hole in the middle of his living room and filled the hole with spikes and all kinds of sharp and pointy items. He covered the hole with palm leaves and an old carpet. Soon as he was done, came a knock on the door, louder and louder.

'Nene, Nene, I know you are in there, open the door! Nene, I know you are in there, open the door! Tua, open the door, I know you are hiding my wife!'

Once the door was opened, Tua said, 'I am your in-law, please show me some respect.'

'Did you see my wife'? Maty removed his shirt and was ready for a fight. 'Did you see my wife?' Maty pushed Tua into the house.

'Please sit down, let us just have a glass of palm wine.'

Maty breathed in, he relaxed a little and walked towards the chair in the middle of the room. As his full body weight reached the chair, Maty fell into the hole. He was pierced and suffered a burst artery, Maty bled to death.

A few days later Tua was summoned into the village hall and was charged with murder by the elders.

'When you see a woman running, know the end of the man is nigh.'

Hans Ndah Nyaa

Four Poems

DISARM

Spit on your very rifle!
Curse the battles.
Rush back to Dialogue where peace abounds.
Return to Reconciliation where meaning abound.
Ponder how much peace hides in peace.
Hide then in the rock of peace,
Where the bullets of war and terror can't penetrate.
In that sturdy rock of peace, love and progress you'll
      meet.
A delectable company there, they'll keep you.

MY NEIGHBORS ALL SWARMING TO THE WEST

'It frustrates staying here!' Tender Africans complain.
Lincoln's and the queen's home spill comfort and riches!
My roof leaks terribly – this I know.
But I'll rather toil to mend my roof,
Than to shamelessly patch-up
Under Lincoln's or Elizabeth's roof.

BREATH COMETH INTO THE DRY BONES IN THE MORNING

"What's noble about Africa that's worth talking about?
Poverty, misery, corruption, war and drought
Constitute Africa's password. I hear that there, all's dry!
Just a few or nothing good to jot on Africa the last
          chapter!"

In my consciousness, this comment burns like flowing lava
Burning and consuming anything on its way.
Like the bones in the valley of dry bones we may be dry,
But dry we'll forever not remain.

Flesh these bones will wear in the morning.
Breath these bones will have in the morning.
Then with wings like eagles we'll soar
And new horizons we'll explore.

Unconsciously, those who render us dry will open
          wide their mouths;
Unconsciously, those who consider us dry bones will
          open their mouths
On seeing the blessings God will accord us with.
Their mouths they'll open till houseflies and envy will fly
          in.

A yellow future we have and in God's hands it is.
Soon our stream of prosperity will be unleashed.
In the morning breath cometh into the so called dry bones,
And a place to be shall be our very home.

WIN BACK OUR ESCAPEES

Dear! Spare me if an escapee I brand thee.
Escapees without blemish thou art.
Paradoxical it is
To watch the innocent fleeing to refuge safer
While heavy-weight culprits
Saunter arrogantly and unperturbed with laws in their
    hands.
Our hands we shouldn't fold and allow these felons go
    unrestricted.
Verily, verily unto you I say!
Just a handful of unarmed but protected robbers
Holding high offices, residing in high quarters, drain
With impunity the dividends of the labour of our
    hands.
From my bowels, deep from my marrows comes this
    truth.
On the streets of Africa just take a look.
Look at the myriad of limousines,
And other automobiles,
Peep in to the residents of our unarmed but protected
    robbers,
Then return and tell me whether a motor park of costly
    cars
they harbour in their enclosures or not.
Adjacent such residents, you find multiple hurt-like
    houses of have nots,
With myriad of them held captives by pauperization.
Very bitter is the nitty-gritty that the wealth of our
    nations

By few unarmed but protected robbers in high places is
        squandered.
In plenty food you find but folk perish in hunger.
Folk are thirsty but everywhere water you find.
The key of our barn and tank by the spoilt is kept.
Artificial scarcity – a stark reality it is today.
The cheated masses at all cost toil to escape
To anywhere, anyhow (mostly to alien regions across
        the seas)
Where barns and tanks there aren't completely keyed.
Available is a single key to open our barn and tank.
We need not pass a special command
For this key to us to be given.
Free of charge we can take, use and own it.
Good governance the magic key is.

Open our barn and tank then – our escapees will return.
Unarmed but protected robbers will face the law.
To escape from here, none will have a cause
Because the treasures we escape to grab abroad,
Right at home we'll find in good measure.
Unbar the barn!
Unbar the tank!
Only to a few it belongs not.
To all it belongs.
Unbar the barn!
Unbar the tank
So that he that labours will starve not
And he that snores while others toil will eat nor drink not.

Prudentia Binwi Asobo

The *Tekumbeng* Parade

It was on a Saturday morning at the brightest hour of the day; the town by some mysterious alchemy assumed a different character. It was almost as if the town set has been changed by some theatrical hand and the daily activities of people altered. The people who ambled round its sunny streets had escaped after news of the *Tekumbeng* parade was announced. Tanyu had left the family compound soon after 10am and wondered into the town at a distinct Saturday morning pace, looking at business men and traders shouting for customers.

Tizihmbu'uh had spent a pleasant thirty minutes doing nothing. Though he had his grandfather's old album in front of him and starred wide at his pictures since the sixties, his mind's eye saw different images. He recalled an instance before he went to college when his grandfather visited them in Hamburg with *kikôunɘ* (Pinyin biscuits: boiled and well dried sweet potatoes cut into tiny slices) and they were at a beach chewing them. He recalled how he told him and his father: "Our culture is the pride of our native people. We must promote and uphold our culture, for a man without culture is no man in our community.

"My children, never allow any man no matter who he is to define you. Be proud of the *Africanity* in you and never allow anyone discourage you. Have more confidence and be shameless to teach them your culture too. Be smart, wear Africa where ever you go, never give up telling them who Africans are; don't care about their opinions that Africa is uncivilized. Nobody should make you feel like your culture is inferior.

"When I was growing up, the Basel Missionaries always told us that their God is superior and very perfect. Well, we didn't argue their teaching, or change from our own worships completely. We worshipped their God no doubt, but when it comes to worshipping our own gods and pouring libation, my father and uncles didn't hesitate".

As Tizihmbu'uh's thoughts wondered about this, he brought his wrist watch round to look at the time when suddenly some men opened the wooden gate and crept in stealthily; two men wearing jumper and shorts topped with faded black caps. It was his Grandfather and one other man. They were all *chop chairs* I think so. They came running towards him and whispered his name sharply, moving closer to him.

"No fear, Tizihmbu'uh, no fear," they commanded. "Tizihmbu'uh! Tizihmbu'uh, leave that place at once, get up and enter the house, don't even try to get out of this fence like you will get into trouble. Those *Tekumbeng* women are out. Yes they are out again; this time as they came to this world," his grandfather shouted.

Tizihmbu'uh got up trembling. He had a sip of *muluh mifuə* (white mimbo) but felt no better. Taking his grandfather's hand in his, they went to the shed near where the goats sleep.

"Grandpa, come and sit down beside me. I don't

know what you are talking about. I can even see you bleeding. What happened to your leg?" Tizihmbu'uh asked in panic.

Tanyu couldn't sit outside. He insisted they get into the house, ran straight to his sitting room and fell on a sofa his son sent to him, shouting at Tizihmbu'uh to shut the door.

"The *Tekumbeng* women have launched an inaudible walk across the silent streets of this town. Women out of the ordinary, women who had been given an insight into something close to the *ikum samba* (the seven king-makers in Pinyin; men enveloped with the spirit of *kwifor*; the most dreaded group of men in Pinyin); a post-menopausal group of women that constitute a powerful secret society, always with bare bodies rubbed with camwood, with *Nkeng* leaves held tight with their lips and their tired breasts resting on their hips. They usually go out with red *awandos* just at the knee level but this day, they dressed like Eve in the Garden of Eden; they tied just dry plantain leaves round their waists so that it falls on their thighs to cover their private parts. It was said that if their mission is very serious, they don't even put on the *leaves*; they go out in total nakedness. With camwood rubbed all over their bodies waving *nkeng* leaves with their left hands and a walking stick on the right hand; the women paraded the streets moving towards *Ntoh Pinyine*" – Tanyu explained.

"They are the most dreaded when it comes to the traditional womenfolk; charged with feeling of anger, unaffected by politicians and social change, the

160

Tekumbeng women usually march to denounce certain issues. Their parades are unperturbed by those who know who they are; their dressing captures the richness of African culture. Hot blood boils in them once they step out on a parade. They were Papa Power's guards in the early 1990s when multiparty politics was at its peak in Cameroon," Tanyu added.

"A wonderful scene truly!" Tizihmbu'uh exclaimed.

"We must be careful the next time *Takumbeng* announces their parade," the other man said, shaking with fear. There was a short silence as the men struggled to catch their breath. The other man looked at Tizihmbu'uh, gave a queer gulping sound in his throat and said:

"My son, we just escaped the dreadful *Tekumbeng* parade. We ran away blindly only to get away anywhere. The penalty of seeing these women naked is death. Their strange costume and unmasked faces is not worth looking at."

"I left home not knowing the *Tekumbeng* women were out. I walked a few paces when I heard women and men running and shouting. Suddenly I saw a long line of people brandishing nkeng leaves in the air; then it dawned on me that the *Tekumbeng* women are out. Thank God the clouds blurred my sight and I didn't see them," Tanyu said. "Two men brushed past me. I turned to my left and right, no wall to flatten myself against and wait till they were out of sight. My heart jumped and then almost stopped beating. I had to find my way out, running forward to see if I could see a place to hide. I didn't seem to be making much progress; I felt tears actually coming to my eyes because I know the penalty in case I see these women."

He glanced at his grandson and limped towards him dripping with sweat. Tizihmbu'uh kept quiet and tried to bring down the fear in the two old men. He feared they could faint. He comforted them with soft words and left them to rest. As he sat outside, so many rhetorical questions ran through his mind:

"Was Peter Mark right that African culture is barbaric and must be wiped away? How can old women parade the streets stark naked? How can grandmothers show their stripped bodies in public? See what they just caused? See how my grandfather is bleeding? Was he even supposed to run away from those women? Couldn't he just stand while they do their crazy parade?"

At about 6pm when birds started flying back to their nests and fowls returning home, all the villagers went out of their hiding places. Tizihmbu'uh waited till the other man left for his compound. He called his grandfather out on the veranda. It was the first time Tizihmbu'uh had confided to anybody since he came to Cameroon; and there was a problem that caused him to open to his grandfather. Standing near his grandfather's bamboo cupboard, his elbow resting on it, in a low tune he said:

"I am sorry to say this about my teacher in College, but I have to do so to clarify my doubts," Tizihmbu'uh said. "Tanyu, grandpa," Tizihmbu'uh called.

"Yes."

Tanyu nodded at him. (A habit of his.)

He moved closer to Tanyu and slowly rubbed his shoulder, imagining how he would start his interrogations.

"Do you know why I have been feeling unhappy ever since I came to Cameroon?" he asked.

"No, my boy, please tell me," Tanyu replied.

"I had a very poor impression about Africa ever since I was in kindergarten. My teachers once said Africans and their culture is barbaric, they are lazy, Africa is poor and everybody there is a beggar and there is always conflict, people being killed every day and they don't work; all they do is stretch their hands to the outside world begging for salvation. He said young kids die from malnutrition, no clothes to wear and no shelter and I believed all he said. Whenever my father said he was coming home, I was always afraid that he might come and die as well," Tizihmbu'uh said.

His grandfather's head jerked upwards and they were staring at each other, and then he closed his eyes as he nodded his head. He put his hand to his head. He swallowed deeply before he shouted: "Cruelty! Cruelty! Peter Mark does not know what he is saying?"

"What do you mean by cruelty? Huh? See the way you were palpitating in the morning. Will this so-called culture pay your medication?" Tizihmbu'uh shouted as well.

"I forgive you because you were born and bred in Germany. You may not know the impact of seeing those women in their naked parade," his grandfather replied.

He swallowed again, and his voice sank to a murmur

as he asked in some panic:

"What made him say that?" Tanyu asked.

His eyes were lost again, his face screwed up pulling his lips from his teeth. His words came as a shock to his grandfather. His eyelids rose, his gaze tight and deep, fixed on Tizihmbu'uh's face. You could see tiny beats of sweat on the faint line of stubble on his upper lip. He wished he would say something good. His Adam's apple jerked up under his chin and fell again, and then he said softly:

"Do you know something T'boy?"

"No Grandpa". Tizihmbu'uh shook his head in refusal.

Tanyu stood up, held his grandson's hands waving in front of him, and then dropping them to his sides, as he said thickly:

"Never allow anybody define who you are. The Whiteman cannot tell your history better than me. The Whiteman knows that Africans are good only for physical work and not capable of doing anything. You, *you* must tell Peter Mark that Africans are not animals; I mean you should let him know that before the imperialists came to Africa, Africans had a religion and a culture they are proud of till date.

"What I mean is, tell Peter Mark that Africans are not barbaric. You can never understand because you were brought up in Europe," Tanyu said.

He dropped on to his knees holding Tizihmbu'uh's hands tightly to his breast, his face bowed over them and his lips were on them. He stood up, walked around the sitting room, one hand running through his hair, the other rubbing the front of his shirt, muttering almost incoherently.

Tizihmbu'uh was gazing at his discouraged face. He sat down, pulled Tizihmbu'uh's shirt and asked him to sit near him. Sitting buttock to buttock, he took his left palm into his, cleared his throat and said:

"Your teacher will always give you a bleak image about Africa. He is not African and has no reason to celebrate Africa. That doesn't affect my person, you know, nothing can remove *Africanity* from me," Tanyu said in a very low tone.

"My boy, do you see me as a lazy person? Have you ever seen me or your grandmother idling around, even though we are of age?" Tanyu asked.

He hurried towards his bed, sorted among the old pictures, then picked out one and handed it to him saying: "That is Africa speaking; that is Cameroon speaking; that is Bamenda speaking." Tanyu knew that pictures would clarify his doubting grandson better than his words.

"Have you seen? Africans are not lazy as the Whiteman thinks. See that picture; that is PRACED CAMEROON – an association of Cameroonians who help educate kids and develop society. Have you seen in pictures how they moved around sensitizing people on the importance of culture, education and agriculture? We had a meeting here and a delegation from this association was sent to us. That was the day I knew people are fighting to celebrate Africa, make food available on all tables. How on earth can your teacher say Africans are lazy?" Tanyu asked.

"What does PRACED stand for?" Tizihmbu'uh asked.

"Prudent Association for Children's Education and Community Development. It has its head office in Bamenda," Tanyu replied.

"Okay, I remember. I saw them on TV on World Aids Day 2016 at the Bamenda ceremonial ground. They even moved from shop to shop in the market sensitizing people how to stop the spread of HIV/AIDS. Does it mean they sponsor kids too?" Tizihmbu'uh asked.

"Yes. It's a non-governmental organization, a group of philanthropic Cameroonians who take care of orphans and the needy. There are so many of such associations in Cameroon. They do their utmost best to show the world that Africa does not depend on Europe for livelihood," Tanyu replied.

"That is exactly why I'm confused here grandpa. I hear men as early as 5am talking and going down those palm bushes and by 8am I see them coming back with their trousers wet up to the knees. Most of them carry bamboos on their shoulders with calabashes on them," said Tizihmbu'uh.

"Look at my hands, feel my palms, see how rough they are; when I was young, that is what I did as well. My health for now doesn't permit me to leave home as early as 5am but my cutlass is my companion. I always go to ŋkarə to tap palm wine to sell to those traders who come from Bamenda. I use the money to buy my medication, palm oil, Maggie and salt. I make sure I give your grandmother oil every month," Tanyu replied.

He liked Tizihmbu'uh. He liked him because he was intelligent but was a little afraid of him perhaps because he saw him as not quite a lover of African cultures. In fact, it was this very fact which prevented him from visiting when there was the *ilerə* in Pinyin. There was a lot of his teacher Peter Mark in him. He had the feeling they could disagree on so many things since he was intoxicated by him.

Tizihmbu'uh was silent for some time. Later, he told Tanyu that he was going to drop Peter Mark's ideas in a bottomless pit.

"I will not allow them assimilate me. Not now when I can understand," Tizihmbu'uh said.

Tanyu smiled at him:

"Have you now realized yourself? You cannot keep away from your culture or tradition and live. Haven't you seen that when they cut the branches of a tree it stays fresh; but when you cut the roots it dies? It is the same with culture and tradition. A man without his culture is no man in our community. Didn't you hear about what happened in Bamenda in the early 1990s when multiparty politics were just starting in Cameroon? So many uniform officials died. They didn't know that men were not supposed to see or touch the *Tekumbeng* women. They pushed them with their guns and even kicked their old buttocks. Some got wounds on their knees while others sprained their ankles. I pitied those young officers because they were all uninformed of the power of *Tekumbeng*," he concluded.

Tizihmbu'uh held his grandfather on his left shoulder, gripped his right hand and brought his forehead closer to his; squeezed his hand again for close to ten minutes and tears rolled down his cheeks.

"I shall not allow anybody condemn my culture as Peter Mark did. I shall always argue with him, even if he gives several reasons to support his point."

It seemed the very air around them had weight and meaning, and every whirling atom had particularity and portent. They were so much in love with each other at that moment that everything they said, everything they did, everything that surrounded them, their entire context had resonance and purpose. Tizihmbu'uh brought his head towards him but didn't speak for a moment.

"I'm… I'm going to take a university course in culture and languages. I've been thinking about this though I wasn't settled. I should let Peter Mark know that Africans have a culture; that they had a language of communication even before they came to Africa. See the many languages Cameroon has? Up to two hundred and fifty, with multiple cultures!" Tizihmbu'uh exclaimed.

"Now you are talking! This is my grandson talking! This boy has African blood in his veins and shouldn't be westernized," Tanyu said aloud.

Tanyu brought himself to the edge of the chair, joining his hands on his laps, he asked cautiously:

"Do you know the Head of State created a commission for multiculturalism and bilingualism in Cameroon? This is to show you how important culture is; for a man without culture is no man in our community," Tanyu repeated.

Tizihmbu'uh put his hand over his face and laughed.

"I've heard, grandpa. I now understand your everyday cry to my father. I shall not give Peter Mark or any of my friends in Hamburg the opportunity to look low on my culture and roots; thank you so much for forcing my father to send me home. I am going back to Hamburg as a Proud African."

Julia Forster

Two Poems

TO MY BEAUTIFUL RASCAL

She's Queen of the castle in Croesor
on an outcrop of rock for a second
before falling twelve feet, head last,
and landing in sheep poo on her shoulder.

I'd refused to race to the silly summit;
my boots from Betws were box-fresh,
to be broken in, but watch me sprint
now towards Matilda Hope!

My fingers trace her skull for lumps,
check for fractures on all four thin limbs –
then spine – then neck. I nurse her head,
her auburn hair, between my trembling hands

and scan her pupils' measureless depths.
You will fall, and fall further, daughter;
your landings will not always be so soft,
but may you always be cherished just like this.

IF 2CVS COULD SPEAK

Peel back my stripy roof; electric ones are for sissies.
We shall make it to eighty, outclass Maseratis
even out-vogue the nearest Range Rover
with my *je ne sais quoi:*
for *deux chevaux* were off-roading
well before those SUVs showed up.

Overtaking a Mercedes Benz will be a breeze –
downhill and with the wind behind us.

Please, let's demonstrate the metal
that rusty Citroëns are still made of.

Casia Wiliam

Five Poems

DIB DAB

We were crossing a field,
heading towards that old lady's house.

She had a sweet shop
in the front room.
Do you remember?
Arm in arm, we'd trot,
conversation bouncing like Dib Dab.
The buttery sun on our backs.
We'd just had our BCGs
so we'd slap each other's
shoulders, for fun.
And now I'm a mum and so are you
and we never see each other,
but our summer days,
that one and a hundred like it
are still a part of me.
The sugar rush of growing up
the way we did,
so quickly,
so free.
Every now and again I feel it,
a syrup-thick kick in my veins
and I'm thirteen again, crossing a field,
not thirty changing a nappy.

LLONYDD

Ar goll yn y ffrae sy'n mynnu
chwarae tic yn fy mhen
mae'n cymryd amser i mi dy glywed.
Rwyt ti'n dangos ffawydden i mi,
ei mes, ei dail main,
dy lais yn dawel
fel yr egwyl rhwng penillion emyn.
Yna'r ysgaw, ei flodau plu eira
a'r coed cyll. Yli, meddat ti,
cynffonnau ŵyn bach, gan osod un
ar gledr styfnig fy llaw.
Cerddwn, gan adael i'r dydd
ddiosg ei hun oddi arnom fesul awr,
a rhywbryd ar hyd y llwybr,
doi a fi eto yn ôl at fy nghoed.

CIP SYDYN

Yn dyner, dawel daw i'r sgrîn
dy lun, mewn du a gwyn.
A gwelaf, mewn hanner curiad
adenydd glöyn byw
dy lygaid a dy gysgod,
dy straeon a dy chwerthin,
dy enw a dy hoff si-hei-lw.
Fel petai rhywun
wedi gosod y cyfan
yn barsel annisgwyl
ar riniog fy myd.
Cyn i eiriau'r nyrs ddisgyn
yn araf amdanaf fel plu,
a ngwneud i'n slwj o eira oer.
Does dim parsel na glöyn byw.
Mae'r llun yn deilchion.

SNOW

When it fell again, snow, in March,
like a friend's Dad in a dressing-gown,
a strange, unexpected sight,
there was a night
when you didn't come home.

One night, and one morning,
when, without warning
I was forced to imagine everything
without you.
Breakfast, lunch, dinner for two.
Hours later, still no sign.

Then it was work, nursery
managing from A to B.
And then Christmas,
his second birthday,
our anniversary.
My whole life fell around me,
cold and pale, like snowflakes.
Our son warm in my arms.
Staring out at black crows
and smiling for him,
a strange calm smothered me.
It was hours later,
after the hugs and the tears
and the shouting and slammed doors,
it was only then that I remembered.
Those perfectly formed snowflakes
that chilled me to the bone.

TRUGAREDDAU

Mae'r cwbl yma o hyd.
Ar ôl blasu llwch y safana,
gweld y lleuad o Bolgatanga
a'r haul mwll yn llosgi'r tir.

Adra, fel petai dim wedi newid,
mae'r cwbl yma o hyd.
Sgarff, gemwaith, llyfrau,
peiriant gwneud smŵddis a ffilmiau,
pentyrrau, pethau. Llond gwlad o drugareddau.
Fi bia'r cwbl?
Dwi'n trio cofio wrth fwytho cotwm a chlawr.
Yn trio clywed y carolau eto, blasu'r twrci, y miri.
Ond yng nghanol fy nyth clud
dwi'n sownd dan swyn Affrica.
Ac mae'r ddynes hudolus honno
a'i dawnsio gwyllt a'i thraed budur,
ei phatrymau lliwgar a'i dwylo gwag
wedi disbyddu pob ystyr o'm eiddo.

Igbokwe Manka'a Mercy Ulomachi Shu

Two Poems

CHILD AT 21

Child at 21
As grey as time,
Mortal stars rise and fall,
Ageless as the sun,

Child at 21,
You have come of age,
As youthful as the month of May,

Knowledge at hand,
Time races fast,
Illimitable as boundless sea,

A vast globe keyboard away,
Complacent cat,
Life passes by.

Ambitious lad,
Insightful ignorance,

Ages foreshadowed,
Best of times,

Perilous,
On a globe's stage,

Systems crack,
Costly better days,

Rules made,
Rules broken,

As broad as Heaven's expanse,
Dance of Century's blues,

Child at 21st,
As a care free wind,

You've come of age,
Child of 21.

HOUSE

Pregnant with abilities,
Blue skies hold great beauty,
A search within to click,
An unknown land ready for discovery,
Behold pearls that breed elegance,
A house lights up to flourish,
Clocks at steady pace as time glows,
Destiny's direction does feet head,
Hold back not in ignorance,
Expressions of joy,
Within bosoms fire be kindled,
A house basks great light,
A house bright in measures,
All awake at heart of night,
Fountain overflow,
A place of plenty,
Chance to chase a quarry,
House of abundance on rest,
Sun rises and sets,
In fullness of time unfolds time,
Great quest to ultimate,
Hands hold great ventures,
Hope to attain wholeness,
Sing with an attitude of X factor,
Oversteps in x-ray,
Deep beyond a yardstick,
Escapade upon great zeal.

Collins Tometi

Where Shall He Run To

Where shall he run to

everywhere he goes
those he does not know demands his life.

He learned to enjoy the company of loneliness,
the mocking laughter of silence he hears,

On his right hand
his brother welcomes him with a dirge
On his left, his pastor rehearses his biography
There in fields faraway lies his memorial tomb
made beautiful by his lover's tears
crying,
who will bury her?

Rudolph Elinge Kange

The Storm Did Not Last

The storm did not last
neither did the sun.

They were here
then no more

I see a future
a harbinger of fears

today it rained
it blossomed

I long for the tears of my youth

O mama Africa
cry thy beloved child

clare e. potter

Two Poems

DIFFINIO

> *A boundary is not that at which something stops …*
> *but is that from which something begins its presencing*
> – Heidegger

Parish-shaped maps
capture moments in flux;
slippery histories, hard to read
on today's landscape,
lines in fields erased,
boundaries dissolved
 —this far, no further
meaningless now.

A fydd y defaid dal
yn aros lle bu eu hen
famau yn pori
now that the wall
is more *bwlch* than
barrier? They'd be free
to pass ancient peripheries
if they wanted

but this clinging to heft
is instinct. Our desire
to lay claim to land
keeps us penned in,

binds us in grass and *gair*.

In the end, though,
it's the land that claims us.

Diffinio
Defining

A fydd y defaid dal
yn aros lle bu eu hen
famau yn pori

And will the sheep still
stay where their ancestors grazed?

bwlch
gap where the wall has collapsed

gair
word

The heft is the area certain breeds of mountain sheep
become accustomed to; this is passed on through
generations

BIRD PRAYER

i. Buzzard

When she was carrying me, my teen mother,
only coins in her purse, walked over the showfield
where autumn had dragged summer's yolk into
September;

something heavy about her heart, and the warm
buzz of fear at what stretched out before her
was left in the grasses, released on her gasp

as three buzzards apostrophised the sky,
their cries declared the mines closed, the land
now free, so they could hunt again, and feed their
young.

ii. Boncath

Welsh for buzzard, I learned, as I was carrying
my girl and one pinned her cries to the sky
above our house. If I pegged washing, she
appeared, and when I sat on a deckchair
practising birth-breathing, she glided.

As I contracted in the bedroom
no panic set in; distress warded off
as I rolled my pregnant self in increasing
circles, mandala-making, remembering
the patterns I'd seen her show in flight.

When our baby was born, the roof of our house split
with buzzard call.

I've not heard her. I've not seen her since
—except when my little girl sings, or, like now
she's jumping on the trampoline as snow falls

and there's a moment when the gap between
going up and coming down . . .

there, in that gap she soars.

Isabel Adonis

The Sweetie Shop

This is what my Mam was like. She would get up every morning and take a bath in an inch of water. She made it hot, all hot. She got in quickly so as not to let the water go even just a bit cold. I think she will burn her feet when I hear her go aaah! in a long suspiration. This was the temperature of the water and not some sensual relief. Almost as soon as she was in the bath she was out; there was no hanging around enjoying herself or anything like that. Then she was out and rubbing herself hard dry; she didn't go for soft towels: and if I was around she would offer me her water which was by then just right and deliciously warm and all soapy with Fairy soap and occasionally some Lux soap flakes.

Dressed in the same old woolen dress that she'd bought in the sale in Marks, a dress that was routinely darned and in the most beautiful way of course – for she was an artist at that, she would rush downstairs to clear out the grate. I don't think she hesitated for one moment, after sleep, not looking round once. She had a long red handled broom for this task. First, she would pull off the front, dragging it and making a terrible noise. I couldn't stand that. Then she would clear all the ashes from underneath the fire basket and place them in a piece of newspaper, which she would wrap up carefully. The red broom which was about twenty-four inches long would be thrust up the chimney in the same way that she cleaned the inside of a chicken at

Christmas, her Marigold hands urgently seeking any soot hanging about up there.

This task complete, she would put the grate back together again noisily and go out to the back yard to collect the small bucket she kept there for washing the tiles on the grate, which she would do next because her life depended on it.

Then, as if she were following some inner dictum, she would put the seersucker tablecloth on the dining room table - it was kept in the second drawer down. In the first drawer was the bone cutlery that you weren't allowed to put in water, not that there was much of a chance of that; she wouldn't let anyone near the dishes. The table laid, she would disappear into the kitchen, put the kettle on, and make a cup of tea.

"A panaid," she would say, "and a smoke". And then call her daughters to get up.

It was Saturday morning about ten o'clock. I was sat at the table - the last one, still playing with my plate. We'd had bacon and eggs that morning as a treat. Mam had sent me the day before to get two slices of bacon from Mrs. Dryherst Denis at the corner shop. "Put it on the book, "she said. When we had bacon, she would grill it slowly, so it didn't crisp too much. She would cut up the two pieces she always bought with a scissors, into six equal pieces. "So, you all get a taste." And there was always an egg of course from the man who brought vegetables to the door." She always cut the white bread for toast in the Welsh way- cut thin and across for sandwiches and cut down thickly for toast.

I was lingering, savoring the taste of the marmalade and bacon because 1 wanted it all to last for ever and ever and it was a nice day that day and I looked at mam through the door and into the kitchen and I said: 'You know mam, when I grow up I want to be a sweet shop lady.' I watched and watched, as I sat at the table, and I was so excited and happy, but she didn't look at me because by now she was on job four, or even five on her internal and eternal list of jobs to get done.

"Washing up." she always said, "is the most important job in the house." She was always saying this, and I suppose she meant it. Servant of servants, she lovingly stacked and washed each plate and rinsed each one; each piece of cutlery was individually washed and placed carefully on a tea towel to be dried and put away.

I said, "mam, mam, I want to be a sweet shop lady" but the kitchen was silent as she bent over the dishes in silent prayer.

"Clear the table and go down to Dunphy's and get some bread." My reverie shattered, I rose in reluctant obedience and took my plate to the kitchen. I returned to shake the tablecloth in the yard: folded it and returned it to the second drawer.

"Take 2/6 from my purse and get a tin loaf and a small Allinson loaf from Needham's," she said without looking.

Maenan road was quiet and it was a nice day too. I crossed over the Conway road by the telephone depot. I didn't understand what went on there except that it was something to do with telephones. We'd just had ours and the number was 75065; it was printed forever on my brain like those jobs that mam did all the while. And then I watched the wind in the trees at the Lady Forester's Home because I had had this idea that when the wind blew that that was God secretly talking to you. Now that was because I had read this poem called 'Who has seen the wind?' in a book that my dad gave me when he came from Africa once. That's what I thought this poem was about

and God was always speaking to me because of that poem.

It was Saturday morning, so the plant nursery was open, and Mr. Roberts was there, though he didn't see me as I passed. I watched my feet and I watched the shapes in the pavement like I was dancing or something. I started to dream my dream about having a sweetie shop and I tried to remember all the different sweets I would have there. I made a list in my mind like the one that mam had in hers.

Boxes of liquorice with Catherine Wheels and white chocolate buttons with hundreds and thousands and the brown chocolate ones, Rowntree's Pastilles and Fruit Gums, and those little boxes of them of course. Mars Bars, because mam liked those, and Milky Ways and all kinds of Cadbury's chocolate, the penny bars and the tuppenny bars and the sixpenny bars. I would have to get Bourne-ville bars with the red wrappers because daddy liked those. There would be scented sweets for the old ladies, Cachous and Scented Violets. Everton Mints and Sharps Toffees, Lemon Bonbons, Mint Imperials and sugared almonds. And Nuttals

Mintoes for Auntie Maggie, I mustn't forget those.

The man behind the counter in Dunphy's knew me. He was tall with a brown cotton coat and grey hair. The counter was polished wood and I put my 2/6 down, and while he went in the back for the ordered bread I played with my feet, moving from one to the other like I wanted to go to the toilet, except that I didn't. I looked at the wood shelves, which went high up, to see how many things I could see.

I saw Uncle Ben's rice in an orange box – mam got that, and I saw all the biscuits in tins – bourbons and custard creams and ginger nuts. Mam didn't buy biscuits much. I could see the Stork margarine and the Welsh butter and that big red machine that they used to cut their bacon and ham. I was frightened of that. Then the man with the grey hair returned all at once and I stopped shuffling and wat-ched him wrap my bread carefully and quietly in tissue paper, the edges curled quickly in his long bony fingers.

"One-and-three," he said so politely and slowly, and I gave him the 2/6 which was dry by now after me getting it all sweaty in my hand. And after giving me the change I said 'bye' and went across the road, past a few shops. Then I saw Mrs. Akie's shop and I noticed her pink nylon coat. She had grey hair too and was shuffling about like me behind her own wood counter. In the back of the shop I just caught a glimpse of Mr. Akie whose face was all pink next to his white hair. He had a pair of scissors in his hand because he was cutting an old man's hair.

I looked quickly in and went on past to Needhams,

just as mam had said. "Could I have a small Allinson's please?" I said, like I was ever such a good girl, being so polite and all. She said, "that will be tenpence-ha'penny," so just as I had calculated I had four pence ha'penny change, and after that I felt truly happy like I had a ticket to go to Rhyl Fun Fair.

So, I left the shop with my two loaves of bread in a string bag and I walked slowly back to Mrs. Akie's, which I knew was the best place in the world to be. I tried not to notice what was going on in the back of the shop because Mam always said that the worst thing imaginable was a man shaving. So being a good girl I had to agree that it was the most 'disgustingest' thing ever. I pretended I didn't notice that pink stuff by the big mirrors in the back because Mrs. Akie said, hello and smiled at me: of course, she knew full well what I wanted.

So, she stood behind her wooden counter, which had all kinds of things on it, like packets of razor blades - seven o 'clock was the cheapest and you got five in a pack. I knew this because I had bought them for daddy when he got back from Africa. I think she had Park Drive Cigarettes and Senior Service and Players Navy Cut too.

But what my lips and mouth longed for was on the other side of the shop behind the main display of sweets. Mrs. Akie's let all the children go behind the counter. I took a quick look at the four big pennies and the ha'penny in my hand, which was getting all wet again, then I just relaxed as I entered my own heaven, like mam did when she was doing the washing up. All in front of me were all the things I loved the most. I clutched my money tightly and I stared in wonderment at the white sherbet. Next to it the lemon crystals had a rainbow running right through it, all-different from the white sherbet, which frothed up in your mouth. I looked for a long time at the lollies, the round ones and the toffee ones and the blackcurrant ones. The flat ones were the best for sherbet though. I saw the Bassets sherbet fountains, but they were tuppence, and the cough candy twists and the black Kop Kops, which had chewy stuff inside.

If somebody had seen my eyes they would have seen them popping out, but nobody thankfully was looking at me because Mrs. Akie knew exactly what kids like me wanted. She just left you all alone until you were ready: she knew exactly that kids didn't like grownups looking at them and trying to help them or anything like that. She knew, as if by magic, the right amount of time to leave you and then she would say. "Are you alright dear?"

I decided I was going to have two black jacks and two fruit salad chews; that would make one penny. Then I would have one ounce of fairy drops. They were little round fruit drops, you got loads for a penny and she would put them in a cone shaped bag. I waited and waited, and I took my own time, in the dark behind the counter with just a bit of light coming through by the penny bars of Cadbury's chocolate and the Five Boys. I had spent tuppence and had tuppence ha'penny left. I saw the blue and yellow wrappers of Refreshers, those lovely sherbet chews, so I had one of those. They lasted ages and it was lovely when the sherbet burst through into your mouth. That only left a penny ha'penny, so I had two flying saucers for a ha'penny. I couldn't decide if I wanted a penny chocolate or some white chocolate pigs or a blackcurrant lolly. I liked the blue colour of the chocolate wrapper because I had decided that blue was my favorite colour. Mam said that when she went to Woods Colwyn Bay she would buy me a blue cardie.

When Mrs. Akie finally came over to me I had made up my mind that I would have a Cadbury bar. "Are you alright dear?" she said sweetly and kindly and I looked over with my brown eyes into her blue eyes, and it was that look that reminded me that when I grew up, I wanted to be like her and have the right amount of time for children. I felt so happy and rich with my sweeties as I stepped out of my sweetie heaven.

I walked with mam's bread up the Queen's road. I had to decide which I would eat first and that took what seemed like a long time. I ate my chocolate bar first taking off the little bit of blue that was the wrapper and the little bit of foil and I stuck the stick all at once into my mouth. It was only the size of my finger, so I soon gobbled it all up. I was humming and going up and down on the kerb; after which 1 looked very quickly at the face of the little black boy on my black jack, peeled off the wrapper and I ate that too. Then I decided to eat the other black jack quickly too because I remembered that they made your mouth all black and mam would know what I'd been up to. I ate a few fruit drops and then I ate a pink fruit salad chew and then crunched a few more fruit drops. I could hear mam warning me in my head about ruining my teeth, but I didn't care. Then I had another fruit chew and I had reached the Lady Forester's home. Each time I ate something I had to put my bags down and wait a bit. So, I stopped to look at the trees so very tall and dark and they were making strange noises as the wind was passing through and I smiled because I knew God was talking to me and I felt fine. I knew He wouldn't mind me spending the change. When I got to the path near our house I was wondering what I would say to mam, but I didn't really care what she would say, and she probably wouldn't even notice because by now she would be on job number forty-two.

Zillah Bowes

Three Poems

BUSHBABY

I've been waiting waiting
            covered by leaves in a bush
waiting to be rescued

I was born not left in the bush
            my light always green
my view always veined

do you know this one
            yes you'll know this one
if you're a bushbaby too

or if someone bushed you
            brush off the earth girl
brush off the earth.

CAMPION FLOWER

Today I'm windsick,
horizon rollicking,

white petals whipped up
by the tramontane.

I hear distant grass tips,
then suddenly I'm pressed
to thunderous edges.

We all blow in time,
even my stamen,
even the broad plane.

Far away my stem aches.
I glimpse it, upside down –

a green flash – then my crown
bent double, touching dry earth.

FAWN-WOMAN

after Born by Kiki Smith

Today my mother is a deer
and I'm born
quickly,
        head first,
                hands on my chest.

I land sideways,
earth grazes
        my shoulder.

Through stuck lashes
sky skates
        on my down.

I shake a little,
taste my first grass
        in the air.

Where will I be born
        tomorrow?

Nsah Mala

Six Poems

DEDICATION OF CONSTIMOCRAZY

I would have loved to dedicate
This book to young Africans,
Promising flowers in black gardens
Torchbearers of a hijacked,
Kidnapped but possible future.

I would have loved to dedicate
This book to young Africans,
As a blood-sealed oath to end slavery
As sackcloth to entomb Libyan memories
As a verbal mustard seed for our new dawn.

But that wouldn't be enough
Unless I first dedicate it to old buttocks
That have become too familiar with thrones,
Igniting flames of hardships which
Chase out African youths like unappeased ghosts.

I mean tired but unretired chiefs and elders
Fighting over extra kegs of village palm wine,
Counting stolen kola nuts from village farms,
Casting lots over who becomes next thief or chief
While starved black children scamper
With fleshless skeletons onto foreign shores.

Like the village high priest,
I will grind this book on peppered stones,

I will stand on the threshold of our homestead,
Invoke the ghosts of murdered youths,
Empty our cries of frustration into the powder
And blow it into the restless air above
For angels to transport into their heads
So they can rummage the shelves
Of their mental libraries till they find
The dust-coated dictionary of truth,
The timeless encyclopaedia called Conscience
And refer dictatorship
And refer oppression
And refer economic sterility
And refer rest or death.

(*St Andrews, 12 December 2017*)

OUR CHALLENGE

Can someone create
A machine which grinds guns
As cows grind grass
To produce manure for peace?

Can someone create
A machine which breaks bombs
As dogs break bones
To produce food for the underfed?

Can someone create
A machine which mashes missiles
As cooks mash macabo
To produce food for the malnourished?

Can someone create
A machine which grates grenades
As farmers grate garri
To produce more healthy humans?

Once we find these people
We must shield from weapon dealers
As hens shield chicks from hawks
Before they abort their inventions!

(Santiago de Compostela, 25 February 2018)

LAST BATTLE, LAST BURIAL

I heard war songs
And I heard galloping horses
Marching past without swords,
Without spears, without bombs,
Without guns, without missiles.
That was after the battle,
The last battle against arms.

I saw humans feasting
And I saw them sleeping in calm.
I saw Peace lifted shoulders-high
By humans with contagious smiles
Beaming on faces, erasing marks of war.
That was after the burial,
The last burial of weapons.

But I saw this across a distant-near future,
A time whose coming met roadblocks
Erected by billionaire arms-dealers.
A time postponed by greed,
 Repelled by bloodsuckers.
A time fought by fools.

(St Andrews, 13 December 2017)

A COUNTRY

Call it nation, state, kingdom or country.
It doesn't matter; what matters is what it isn't.
A country isn't pieces of cloth on poles;
That's changeable.
A country isn't erasable ink on dusty papers;
That's modifiable.
A country isn't imaginary lines on pages;
That's alterable.
A country isn't a gang of griots singing grandeurs
Of mortal dictators; it's the immortality of its totality.
A country isn't profit-driven sermons from political
        pulpits;
It isn't what ruling minorities conjure.
A country is beyond definition, only people define it.
The term country was born after countries.
A country is its
Whistling winds,
Silent streams,
Waxing waterfalls,
Handsome hills,
Freshening forests,
Merrymaking monkeys,
Sleeping soils,
& prancing people
Who eat from its abundance –
Mindful of their co-inhabitants of the Earth.
A country is a log of wood
Continuously sculpted by its people.
A country is a chameleon

Which wears the colours of its people –
Prominent proportions of its population.
A country shouldn't dance to deceitful drumbeats
Vibrating down from dictatorial altars.

(*Santiago de Compostela, 16 February 2018*)

HER SILENCE

Suddenly she went mute
Like an unmoving stone
Her silence throbbed
Across voids
Asked why, she muttered:
The tree in their yard
Was shaking violently
As angry gusts of wind
Slapped it, blaming it
For identities sliding
Down throats of mambas
Oracles from far and near
Diagnosed its rotting roots
They urged elders to unearth
The tree, balm its sick roots
And replant; but they chose
To prune branches, to caress leaves
As its decaying roots creaked
Underneath, its trunk tilting
In ferocious sways
And she borrowed muteness
From the wise Tortoise
To seek shelter before its fall

(Santiago de Compostela, 8 March 2018)

RWANDA

Rwanda,
A collective wound
Bandaged with forgiveness
Rubbed with love
Healed scar smoother
Than uninjured bodies
Elsewhere in Africa

Rwanda,
They held mourning wreaths,
Inevitable future smiled
Wreaths dropped to hug future
& sprouted into development roses
In a garden that glitters more than
Elsewhere in Africa

But, today we watch
Wide wounds devour
Other limbs of Africa –
Pus stinks below the Fako
Nyiragongo's arms in red
Blood pools in Sambisa
& UN snores in approval.

(*Gisenyi, 20 March 2018*)

Dibussi Tande

Six Poems

MAROUA THE MARTYR

Beautiful offspring of the Sahel
Land of shifting sands and shaded streets
Land of *Bilbil, Couscous* and *Folléré*
Land of overflowing hospitality
Maroua the beautiful
Boko Haram's unwilling lover...

We hear your cries of distress
Echoing across the Mandara mountains
We see your tears of desperation
Flowing down the Mayo Kaliao river
We hear your howls of anguish
Thundering down Mount Maroua
We shudder at the woeful wails
Of your hapless children
As your leaves turn into petals of blood

But do not despair
Cherished child of the Diamare!
From your toil and tears
Shall sprout your freedoms lost
Your broken heart shall mend
Your gentle soul shall heal
And your ghastly scars shall fade
Like a thief in the night

And throughout the ages
The story shall be told
All across this parched
And picturesque land
Of a proud and resilient people
Who rose from the depths of helplessness
To stand tall once again
Like the unbendable Mindif mountain

THE GHOST OF UM NYOBE (AN ODE TO BB)

They say you died in enemy territory
They say you died on the wrong side of THE BRIDGE
But what better place to die
– On the other side of the bridge –
Than in the Sanaga Maritime –
The sacred land of the *Ngog Lituba*
The springboard of Cameroun nationalism
The heartland of the Cameroun resistance;
Purified with the blood of thousands of patriots
Who said NO! to the imperialists and neo-colonialists?

You met your maker at Misole II
Down the road from Boumnyebel –
Birth place of Ruben Um Nyobe
The venerated *Mpodol*
The immortal soul of the *gwet bi kundè*
who is entombed in hallowed ground
in Eseka – still farther down road…

Surely his spirit watched over you
At that fateful moment
Gently guiding you towards your seat
On the pantheon of departed heroes
Where you rightly belong

The sleepy hamlet of Misole II
Is now etched in our collective consciousness
Not as a symbol of death and despair
Not as a symbol of dreams unfulfilled
But as a reminder of battles past
Of battles lost – of battles won

Of battles yet to come;
And a rallying cry
To the Obasinjom Warriors
Who shall restore this land
To its erstwhile glory

Gwet bi kundè – War of Independence in Bassa language

Mpodol – "The Prophet" as the Bassa referred to Um Nyobe, founder of the Cameroonian nationalist party, Union des populations du Cameroun (UPC)

Ngog Lituba – the sacred Rock Cave, the natural and spiritual sanctuary of the Bassa people

THE CITADEL

I

The Mobilization:
The fiery speeches
The protest marches
The huge rallies
The call to arms

The angry cries :
La conférence nationale
il y'aura !!
Fait quoi fait quoi
il y'aura !!
Ça gâte, ça gâte !!
Campus Mort!!!

The irreverent chants:
Mbéré, Mbéré di suffer
Paul Biya di Chop Moni
Small Paul Biya big big tif man
Wandafool!

The freedom Fighters:
Parlement, Powell, Schwatzkopt
Nidal, Samory, Thatcher

The villains:
Délégué, Espion, Auto-défense
Manda Fils, Action Directe

The War of Tracts:
"They have stolen our lands

… and our women!"
"Anglo-Bami Go Home!"

The flashpoints:
Bassorah,
Chateau, Cradat
Carrefour Orly
Sous le manguier
Obili, Mokolo

The violence:
The Ninjas are here!
Run for your lives!
The tear gas and the tears
The blood and the bullets
"le CEPE dépasse le BAC !"
« On va voir qui est qui ! »

The detention centers:
Americanos, GMI
Legion, Semil
Quartier Général
Cinquième…

The wide-eyed denial:
Zero Mort!!!!

II

The unending Misery:
hide-and-seek
with the "bailleur"
to avoid paying rents
SNEC pipes unearthed

SONEL cables cut
– no water no electricity –
but life must go on
in slum city –
Bonamoussadi my love…

Living on the edge:
Epsi pitié…
Pain chargé
Tourne dos
Beignet haricot
"Le Jazz"
Resto… dindon
Survival of the fittest…

III

The decadence:
Women of the night
Desperately hawking their wares
Tycoons in state-owned Pajeros
searching for the elixir of youth
In the dark and dangerous alleys
of the dilapidated mini-cités…
uncaring and treading
where even angels fear…

Partying amidst the squalor:
Pepe Kalle – *Bakuba show*
Zaiko langa – *Nippon Banzai*
Têtes Brulées – *Essingan*
Kassav – *Zouk la sé sel medi kaman nou ni*
Edith Lefel – Frankie Vincent

Zouk Love – Zouk Porno
Nkodo Sitony – *Au Village!!!*
Mbarga Soukous – *"à cheval"*
Essamba! Essamba!
Party like there's no tomorrow!

The loss of hope:
7000 students squeezed into Amphi 700
Travaux dirigés at the *poulailler*
Third World *Doktas*
ranting from the rostrum
and hawking dog-eared polycopies
Le front
Septembriste
Cartouche
Mandat grillé
End of the road...

This is Ngoa-Ekele
Our citadel of learning
The training ground
of "tomorrow's generation"

THE WALLS OF JOHANNESBURG

We are a mirror to the soul of our reborn nation
Reflecting the fears and frustrations of its people.
We are the sentinels of stereotypes that refuse to die
in a nation whose memory is etched in black and white.
We are a reflection of the fading rainbow
slowly dissolving into this concrete divide.
We are the gatekeepers of the New World Order
separating the haves from the have-nots.
We are the unassailable rings of steel
Keeping the undesirables at bay.
We are the walls of Johannesburg
Wishing we did not have to exist...

Inspired by the gated communities in Johannesburg, South Africa.

THE BRIDGE

The bridge...
Ever so steady
Ever so stoic

the bridge...
that enduring link
between the past and the present
the present and the future...

the bridge...
that candid scale
balancing darkness and daylight
despair and hope...

the bridge...
that shiny beacon
pointing towards our dreams
urging us towards our goals...

the bridge...
that all-knowing flashlight
pointing out past mistakes
warning us of potential pitfalls...

The bridge...
Ever so sturdy
Ever so enduring
Ever so illuminating

BREF SEJOUR

It's been a lifetime since he left
for a *bref séjour* across the seas
In his absence the people grope for survival
like drunken sailors staggering in a dark alley
wishing they had a steady and trusted hand
to guide them through these turbulent times
But this matters little to the Prince
For he knows that upon his return
The docile and grovelling masses
Shall welcome him with open hands
grateful that he deigned to return
once again to their cursed land
for yet another *bref séjour*

Jude Emmanuel Kebuma Tita

Small Soppo Water Conflict

Soundless the drums
Still, revolts 'kai water'
Magma beneath boils,
Slowly it boils.

Our ancestors are silent
did they not bring forth our demise?
one side provokes, the other retaliates, a circle, vicious
water brings forth life,
lamentation

The nightingale whispers,
it questions: a life without water?
We call upon you, Wovilla
kai Water may you roar again,
let your children sit around you
may we drink from your bosom plenty
'Moto maimbe' – peace

Mougoué Leuyam

Cry Mother Africa

I went home to see Mama Africa
None was there but 'dem boyz'
Their chorus,
Where is she?

'she gone, can't you see

Silence is the womb
'in solemn, the winds blow from the horn of Africa, to
its underbelly

'Where are thou mother'
I shout to the mountains, calling out the names of my
ancestors one by one.

What happened to the Fighter?
Mourn not, they replied,
'a Hero is resting'

She gave her all,
mother, warrior,
my sisters cried

Tears from dawn till dusk

Crying for those she lost as the war raged within and
without

REST IN PERFECT POWER
MAMA AFRICA

Mesue Lucy Ebude

Two Poems

DIFFERENT

They dislike me,
I'm different.
Not aligned with how society expects me to act.

Fact is they do not know me,
Of that I am certain.

I walk strange,
I talk strange
under the mango tree,

They gossip
See how they gaze

Sometimes I fear
Misconception of most,

A few like sheep condemned me
Before they got to meet me,
To even know me

If we must build, and build we must

Let's accept the rainbow.
One beam of light, different colours,
Beautifully entangled

MY MAMA,

The wiser version of my first X chromosome. As the soil of the earth keeps embracing my extending roots; I carry you wherever I go. Growing from that little girl to a not so little girl anymore even though I know I will forever be your little girl. I remember when these roots of mine showed no progress, made no efforts to grow. You watered me down with love, when water got scares you cried and used your tears, added manure, prayed and hoped I grow. You never gave up regardless of the hard time. My perfect picture of endurance, she is wonderfully made and brave. A proof that true love exists, is my Mama. You are my definition of true love. People say they want a love as big and deep as the ocean, each time I hear that I smile at their ignorance because they know not that a mother's Love is limitless. It has no depth and its size is immeasurable. Even when you called a wrong shot, I see your perspective now, you always called it from the love angle. The definition of true, pure and an unquestionably love. Need I say more, I love that it's you I choose as Mama, and if some theory like the reincarnation truly does exist in the heavens or next world wherever that may be. wait for me I'm coming back, Yes, I'm coming back as your daughter. For there is no other mama, I would rather have.

Efange Protus Esuka

Three Poems

A PLACE OF PEACE

Africans, African! Here is my mountain cave home
        town,
Do I sit at the sobs; eyes all moist and swollen with
        tears,
My pounding, molten heart that has through the years
        known no peace,
Now drags me to a jungle of gloom.

Tell us, all us Africans, about the millions of bones
That has through time been shoveled in mass graves
Statesmen now and then clad in clattering armor,
Get confused no doubt with R.I.P for peace in Africa.

Yet, peace is not in bribery, tribalism, guns or grave
Our once beauteous gardens have all like ghost,
Vanished before our haggard, fleeting, quivering brave,
Africans, how neglectful have we not thought of our -
        children.

All armament industries have we learnt to import
While 'malnutritive' patriotic lips sigh and die of
        hunger
Some egoistic brothers get amused with greed, on the-
        bedrock of chance,
And like weaver birds, destroy what is on hanger

Seeds planted on the manure of African martyrs

Are all ready, for no egoistic 'junggler's' elephant
      shear,
Time it is to squeeze their juice for all to shear,
While we wipe those self-made slippery paths of
      human blood.

Let us all from the surface of the slippery earth,
Wipe the real human blood as we wed between tribes;
Religions, colours, inventing those good sides of
      culture,
For a peaceful more refined world. A place of peace.

(2nd May, 1995)

THE PRIZE FOR AIR.

Who but none,
Can undo this traction
That pulls me to a grave
Not designed for me

Great just too great,
A confusion from tribulations
That swims the sea of pains,
Making the body nominal.

It seems like a trance;
My life, the prize for air
While others breathe with satisfaction
I breathe, with an apology.

WEST COAST BEACHES

Sweet beaches feed my eyes
Calm places so bright and fair
Blue the water as cold as ice
Reminds me of my youth.

When at first, I saw the vast
Place consumed by rain
Of the heat and sun behind
Not in Debundscha it must rain,

Isokolo, Batoke and Bakingili
Isongo, Debundscha to Idenau
The whole of West Coast to Sanje
Is blessed with beaches to see.

I fell in love with the coast
That had a path than road
And to-day like a song
Idenau holds my love song.

(*1984*)

Joffi Ewusi

Six Poems

THE SMILING SUN

Beyond East superlative sun rises.
Shining brightly, she almost dances.
Without a veil, shows her face.
The world could not be a better place.

Piercing her way through clouds so dark,
Scintillating smiling sun shines with a spark.
Confident contentment on her face,
Shinning sublimely with golden grace.

Radiant, dashing, beautiful brilliant face,
Shinning greatly generously far in space.
Possessing an aura of power,
Hovering yonder sky's tower.

Sunlight shimmers on lakes and seas.
Sunny scenic splendours on grass and trees.
No scenery could look more right.
Shinning down the world so bright.

Beyond West, grandeur sun sleeps.
The whole wide world sleeps
When she hides her face.
In a dark, mysterious unknown place.

Bed on which gay sun lies,
Is as flickering as a dice.
Yellow, white, dark, sometimes blue.

Rainbow hues, yet pure and true.

Sparkling youthfully despite the years.
Her bright face shines with no tears.
When misty rain touches her face,
She glows distinctly vividly for life in space.

THE BUTTERFLY

She fluttered in her tiny sundry plumage
Spreading her dainty, playful and cheerful,
Bright brilliant wings,
Flying gracefully from tree to tree
Kissing and sucking softly from flower to flower
Nurturing and maturing her figure.

Preening herself and
Ploughing her way through the misty clouds
Flying higher and caressing the skies
To unknown galaxies and rainbows.
 I want to take a flight with her.
Out of the world, out of sight
To sit on her cheerful dainty wings as
She soars away to gentle dream lands....

SHE WAKES!

O how she slept with a soothing smile.
Like a veil, or rather the mane of a horse,
Silky, ebony lustrous hair cascaded over her shoulders.
Her hazel brown complexion glinted in the twilight.
Sensual curves of a graceful African woman
And the silky softness of her skin
Furnished her an overpowering femininity
With the essence and quintessence of alluring
          womanhood.
Her presence awarded a soporific effect
And drowned me sleeping into oblivion
Shutting out the world.

The fading luminescence of the moonlight
Ushered and graced the bustling dawn.
The relics of the night were restrained
By the beguiling ingress of the fair sun
Ushering bright morning glory.
She stirred and her overpowering smile
Like a galaxy of stars
Serenaded the birds to sing awake the dawn.

Eyelids cascading over her adumbral cheeks fluttered.
At the sight of me, her eyes twinkled and shone like
          pearls.
She smiled again. Her smile was a familiar song.
O how my heart melts with that sanguine
Sublime smile so sweet every morning.
Her eyes dazzle brilliantly like the rays of the sun.
This rejuvenates new hopes for my future.

Her loving arms stretched out to take me home
To the warm embrace; a magic wand
Casting away all my sorrows.

MY CANARY

My endearing yellow canary, my beloved friend,
Wakes me up every morning with her tweet sweet
        melodies
Serenading my sad world with her seraphic splendid
        notes
Thawing my icy countenance with her chirpy jingle.
Her song is chorused by other birds hatching a new day.

My charming canary, my devoted friend,
She fails never to burst my dark world open
With her doting and devoted harmony,
How sweet the music she chirps so gracefully.

Morning fully clad itself in almost pitch darkness.
And the trees cried from the heavy rain.
Even the palm trees bowed with the wind
But my canary was not intimidated!
Her cheerful wings gave a courtly dance to her melody
She pierced her beak on my window frame
And aye, that morning, she sang so sweet.
With her passionate lyrics buried optimistically in her
        throat,
Her twittering melody was lucid and luminous.

I was drawn to the sensuous qualities of her harmony.

I listened enthralled to the assonance of that delightful
    harmony
As my soul joined her melody of joy
And I celebrated the sunrise of a new day.

MOSOLE: THE ENDLESS STREAM

Unfathomable from the opaque volcanic mountain,
    Mosole, the buoyant brook emerged,
    Bobbed and burbled over the slick stones
        Like a hanging waterfall.
    Flowing boldly from grand Fako and
    Trailing its track to the energetic Atlantic.

The dancing, gleaming stream curled and meandered
        like a serpent
And murmured like the ocean waves on boulders.
    Yet it whispered when it surfed gently over tiny
        pebbles.

Flowing boldly, his torrent rippled and blew some
        light petals
That drowned along with him to unknown caves and
        unexplored beaches.
The rapacious wind sought to blow the brook away
But he flowed faster and instead chased the wind away
        with his torrential vigour.

At the fluvial forked carrefour, a languid pool met
With the jovial stream and blended, meshing their
fluids
In a warm embrace; caressing each other.
The overpowering stream possessed the languid pool
and she moaned.
The mysterious communion between both waters
Ignited a more vigorous energy until sparks of foams
And bubbles overflowed; cascading into a waterfall
Where life was born, and fishes swam towards fertile
beaches.

Arm in glove, they flowed faster, faster….
As happy as a fountain, they travelled to the volcanic
shadows and mesmeric sunset Disappearing into the
meadows and flowed a thousand miles into the West
Coast.
Crossing rivers, forests, and reappearing alone,
ravishing everything on his way.

Alas his journey almost ended but not so,
Emptying his contents to the thirsty, famished
voracious Atlantic whose
Water currents almost drowned the brook in a hungry
possession.

MY BLUE ROSE

I planted daffodils, dahlias, and daisies.

At the centre of the garden
Blossomed outstandingly my blue rose
Special in my harem of flowers.

I hailed her in fond appraisal every morning.
Her roots were buried deep in the soil
Her willowy lissom spiky stem bore the curves
Of a feminine African beautiful maiden.

Her branches flourished lush feathery fine foliage.
And my enchanting, bewitching, delightful
Blue rose springing from a bud,
Bloomed bluer than the bluest sea.

My singular blue rose, glorious in her grace and
Rarer than the most priceless precious stone
Gazed at me with glowing petals
And a shivery sensation swept through my spine.

I pruned, watered, nurtured
And adored my budding blue rose.
Protecting her from invaders,
I built a heart shaped fence to guard her.

Going to caress my beautiful blue rose,
I went wild with shock.
I met her uprooted and destroyed.
The jealous flowers watching.

She lay as fragile as a house of cards
Naked, raped, dislocated, and displaced.
My life had just been
Irrevocably altered.

Tifuh Esther

Grandpa's Spirit

Maria and the kids walked briskly on the rugged road that led up the steep hill. It was getting dark and she knew she wouldn't recognize Mammy's house in the darkness. The children stumbled and fell a few times. But, she only scolded and said "ashia" and the climb continued. The houses were all the same. They seemed to have sprung from one hundred years ago. The small houses were closely knit together with very small corridors separating them. They all looked alike. Rusted corrugated zinc from the German era, stood on plank houses. The walls were made of drums which had been flattened and nailed together. Some of the walls had developed tiny holes through which tiny rays of light escaped to the dark outside. The upper parts of the walls were made with planks. Some showed signs that they had been eaten up by insects and may give way anytime. The window had plank louvers. Plywood, evenly cut and nailed together to form louvers that were never opened. The first time Maria had visited Mammy was in the raining season. Layers of moss had coated the zinc and the pavement that led towards Mammy's house. The road was wet and slippery. Now, it was dry and stony.

Mammy was sitting in from of her house when they arrived. She got up with a jerk, held her back and fell back on the chair.

"This back, can't you allow me welcome my grandchildren," she grumbled in Pidgin English.

The grandchildren ran toward her and embraced her. They stayed entwined till Maria reminded them that it was time to go inside the house. Mammy's house was unlike the others. It was a recently constructed brick house. Maria's husband had hurriedly constructed the house two years before. That was when Mammy was very ill, and they had feared she could die. He didn't want people to question why his mother stayed in a wooden shack when he had made of lot of money in the capital of Cameroon. Thank God, Mammy did not die. And, the house had brought a lot of good to the family. Maria could now visit with her children. Something her husband never wanted before now because the children wouldn't have a decent place to sleep or take a bath. Now Mammy had a flushing toilet, a small gas kitchen and cable television.

Grandpa starred at Maria as soon as she entered and sat down. Mammy told the children to stand up and greet Grandpa. The kids turned in bewilderment as if to say; "Where he is?" Mammy laughed and pointed at the photo that stood on the old dust covered cupboard.

"That is your Grandpa," she said.

"But Grandpa's dead. How can we greet a dead person?" they asked but Mammy smiled.

"Your Grandpa is not dead children; he is in this house right now as we are talking,"

"Grandma, don't scare the kids," Maria said and carried their suitcases to the room opposite grandma's room.

"Who wants to sleep with grandma?" She asked aloud. ...there is just one bed in this other room."

She heard the children scream, "Not me, not me," and smiled.

That's the answer she expected from them. She removed Mammy's gifts and carried their suitcases towards her room. The door was half closed and it was dark inside. She changed her mind and reentered the parlor to see Grandpa staring at her. She moved from one end of the parlor to the other end and Grandpa's eyes seemed to follow her.

Maria loved Mammy very much. She was unlike any other mother-in-law. She was so gentle and loving and she smiled at the fact that she had also given birth to and nurtured a very handsome man, her husband and very successful business man.

Maria's husband's success seemed to be reflected everywhere around Mammy's house. It was one of the few brick buildings in the quarter. It had glass windows, a modern toilet and a refrigerator. Maria had also bought Mammy these high-class Nigerian laces that cost hundreds of thousands of francs. Mammy once told her how she was the envy of all, whenever she went for their village meetings. She never stopped thanking her.

"Thank you for my gold jewelry and my leather handbag and slippers, thank you daughter."

Mammy wanted all the changes to happen only in her old house. Maria's husband had acquired land in a chic quarter and had wanted to build the new house there. But, Mammy had laughed at them so hard and said: "My husband left me in this house and he comes from me from time to time. I don't want him to go around looking for me in strange quarters. He married me and brought me here, we had all our kids in this same house. I want that when he comes for me, he should find me here."

The tiredness of the long journey from Yaoundé to Mungo made the children sleep right into the morning. Maria got up early to clean. Mammy had refused the services of a house help. Mammy always said; a woman who had as many grandchildren as she did should not lack a child to stay with. She wanted to stay with one of her grandchildren. Maria had explained to her how parents should be given the opportunity to raise their kids and impact the kind of morals they wanted. Grandmothers petted and spoiled the kids. Mammy's grandson who had been forced by her parents to live with Mammy only slept and ate and never helped the old woman to do chores.

Maria packed a heap of dirty dresses and steeped in a basin. She looked at her artificial nails and hoped they didn't fall off before she went back to Yaoundé. Maria first swept the yard and entered the firewood kitchen to clean. She saw plates and pots with food which had mold growing on them. In Yaoundé, she has two maids and had forgotten how to do such chores. But Maria knew in Africa you need to flatter your mother-in-law to keep your special place in your husband's heart. By the time the children got up, Maria had cleaned the backyard, done the washing and broken her silver nails. She heard voices in Mammy's room and went to see the kids with her.

"Good morning mom," they greeted

"This palace stings," Stacy complained

"Shiiiiiip" she said shutting her mouth

"Breakfast is ready, come with Mammy for breakfast," they scrambled out of the room. Maria served the children and waited for Mammy to show up. Maria wondered what was keeping Mammy in her room for that long. Her tea was getting cold. The door was half shut and she heard her talking to someone. She peeped and saw Mammy sitting on the bed facing the head of the bed.

"The children are here, they came to greet us. Make sure you bless them from above," Maria pushed the door and burst out laughing.

"Mammy, when will you come to terms with the fact that your husband is dead and gone? You are talking to the wind, there is nobody there."

"My daughter, you are young. What my eyes have seen and my ears have heard, my mouth can't talk. Whenever you want to enter my room, always knock; wait a few seconds before you enter. Your father-in-law is in this room."

"Where, I can't see him?" she said looking around.

"He can see you because he is spirit. Just do as I say."

During breakfast Maria kept pondering on what her Mammy had said and as soon as she cleared the dishes, she asked her how her husband had died, was he sick?"

"No, he was not sick; he was a very good man."

"It's been thirty years since he died, do you still

remember him."

She looked at Maria, shook her head and said.

"Thirty years is a long time. But, when you love your husband as much as I did, it's just like it was yesterday. My husband had a friend, a very good friend; he trusted his friend and his friend sold him."

"Sold him, how?"

"His friend had three wives; the first wife gave birth to three children. All the children died in infancy and their father never saw the corpses. He begged my husband to take the corpses to the village and he never turned up to see the children before burial. I thought it was strange and told my husband not to help him anymore. But, he laughed at me and said I reasoned like a woman. His friend's three wives all lost their children and they ran away leaving their husband alone. He went around trying to marry other women. But, all families refused. They had heard about the sudden death of his children.

Then my husband died mysteriously. He was not sick, he just died and his best friend didn't come to see me or the children. Three weeks after my husband died, he bought a car, a brand new Pajero. He never came to see me and the children. We were languishing in poverty and he knew about it. He bought two other cars and went around the town; he never came back to us."

"That's strange but... " Maria said

"Then people started talking. They said they had seen my husband in the north off-loading bags of groundnuts from trailers."

"He was dead."

"Physically…they had transformed him to a zombie slave."

"Why didn't you go and look for him, to see if it was true or false?"

"I couldn't leave twelve hundred children to pursue a mirage. After all the love we shared lives on in my heart. He is still around me."

Maria left the kids with Mammy and rushed to the market for Christmas shopping. She bought just the essentials, the chicken, rice, crackers, popcorn and palettes of juice. She forgot to ask if Mammy had invited guests for Christmas. When she got back to Mammy's house, Mammy was beaming at the Christmas decorations which the children had hung all over. There were banners of merry x-mas and happy New Year. She remembered her well decorated tree at home. The children had hoped they would bring it along so that Father Christmas would visit Mammy's house. But she convinced them that it was of no use. After all, they had bought classy remote-controlled toy cars and boats from the supermarket. And, they never stopped opening the boxes to make sure the toys were still there.

Maria boarded a bike after shopping and bounced all the way home on the rugged road to Mammy's house. Mammy watched quietly as she removed the stuff from two market bags and shock his head.

"What will you cook for us for Christmas?" Mammy asked.

"Jollof rice, I mean special Chinese fried rice. Then, I

will fry crackers, popcorn and buy a cake from the bakery".

"Is it that your husband did not give you enough money for the festivities?" She asked shaking her head.

"On the contrary he gave me a lot of money for the kids' dresses, shoes and toys. Your grandkids will be supper tomorrow. I bought them designers dresses."

"Your young people, she said shaking her head "You don't know how to show love. When my husband was alive, I used to cook four meals for Christmas. He would kill a goat, buy several chickens, pork, fish, drinks and the whole quarter would come and eat at our home."

"Four meals for Christmas, did you have servants Mammy?"

"No servants, I would start cooking on the eve of Christmas. The next morning, my husband would take the kids to church, while l stayed home to complete the cooking."

"Alone! Mammy, so you didn't go to church too? Then how did you enjoy Mammy."

"I used to enjoy a lot. I cooked a variety for foods and served throughout the day. By four pm, the kids would go to town with their Daddy, while I do the washing up and when they came back by six pm, I would take a bath and wear my Christmas attire."

"Woah, he bought you a Christmas dress?"

"Off course, didn't your husband buy you a Christmas dress? These men nowadays don't know how to show love?"

"Mammy, he buys me dresses and jewelry all the

time, especially when he goes on trips abroad. I always have new clothes."

"A Christmas dress is a Christmas dress. As I was saying, after dressing up, he held my hand. We were like a newly married couple and we went to the cinema."

"Woah! Mammy in the sixties? That was romantic."

"That's why our love has never died in spite of his death. Our love was true love. He petted me a lot. They used to call me Madame because I never had a farm. He bought everything for me from the market. I never cultivated like the other women, until after his death. When my husband died, I realized that he had no savings. So, after living the life of a princess, I was left alone with ten kids to raise. And, I didn't even know how to farm. That's the first time I knew that my husband was still in the house because, I borrowed money and bought a hectare of land; then I dreamed how he helped me to work the farm. The next morning, I felt so energetic and strong that I never stopped working on the farm. His spirit got into my body and gave me strength."

Early on Christmas morning Maria hurriedly cooked food for the house and took the kids to church. She imagined her husband in that hall forty years before, with his father and siblings each brandishing a five hundred franc note and Mammy had said. After the church service, Maria carried the baby on her back. Maria heard the designer shoes of her kids stroke the rocky road and it was every minute. The kids had never trod on such a road before. They left their house and were chauffeur driven to a private school and back every day. Maria and the kids met Mammy drying clothes outside. Two sparking white shirts, a trouser and an old suit.

"These were Grandpa's favorite dresses before he died." she said, "I make it a habit to air and iron every Christmas."

"Mammy, please, don't spoil the fun of Christmas. Let's go inside and eat our food. Grandpa is up there being heaven with the angels, singing halleluiah." she joked and they all laughed.

Mammy didn't sleep well that night. She had an asthmatic attack and wheezed all night. Maria heard her wheezing and went to assist her. Maria barely breathed in the stuffy room. It smelt of dirt, damp and she had the smell of dry meat. She wondered if Mammy kept dry meat in her room away from her grandson. Maria decided to air and to clean the room the next morning after Mammy's visit to the hospital. The room needed thorough cleaning.

So, the next morning as soon as Mammy left the house with her grandson for the Doctor's, Maria went straight to work. Maria removed dirty dresses, half dry mildew dresses, left over pieces of fish and meat and small bundles of fried corn and groundnut. Ants had infected them and she wondered why grandma kept them instead of throwing away. She tried sweeping a heap of soil from under the bed. But, the more she swept, the more the soil kept coming. Maria bent low and noticed a heap of earth. She pushed with her hand and noticed it was as hard as a rock, as if it had been molded with water. Maria went to the kitchen and got a hoe and a bucket. The first struck of the hoe created a small hole which Maria widened with her hand. A heap of caked earth fell into her hands exposing two sockets, the same on the photo frame in the living room. She screamed and ran out of the room. She had just exposed a human skull under Mammy's bed. The neighbors came in thinking something bad had happened to Mammy. But, she assured them that all was fine and sat in a corner crying till Mammy returned. When Mammy heard and saw what had happened, she fell to the ground and wept bitterly; as if her husband had just died. Mammy continued wailing throughout the day and refused to eat or drink anything.

Later in the evening, after the wailing and mourning Mammy called Maria into her room in the evening and asked her to apologize to her father-in-law. Maria burst out crying and appealing for forgiveness at the open socket, nose and mouth. At the end of the lamentations, Mammy covered the skull with earth and molded the clay to cover it. Then she explained to Maria that the skull will stay under her bed until she and her husband build a befitting house in the village to house her dear husband's spirit.

Joyce Ashuntantang

Six Poems

MESSAGE FROM BUEA-BAMENDA-MAMFE

Your silence was no alarm song stealing dreams from
my sleep.
The blood on the streets was your letter to me.

The enraged masses became your email.
The dreams on placards twitted your desires...

You are the elephant who comes at the rear of the herd
You are the farmer who fends off birds from your
neighbor's farm

Ah neh nta ya*, I never looked through the door for
your shadow
No true warrior sleeps on his bed when the drums of
war disturb our peace

You belong to the people; I, a servant of the gods
Till the soil where you plant your feet and feed your
soul.

* Beloved

THE CHILDREN OF THE HEARTH HAVE COME

For Anglophone Cameroon Youths in 2017

The Children of the hearth have come.
They have come to reclaim their future.
Their footprints find their marching pair in the
Debris of an almost forgotten story.

They march inside the mansion of their history,
Opening windows into neglected spaces.
Laughing ghosts in chambers of memory
Haunt and mock their indolent present.

Refrain: The children of the hearth have come

They saunter into the kitchen of hidden desires,
Sweeping ashes from fires long extinguished.
Faithful stones of the fireplace re-pay
the debt of stories which must be told.

They follow blood stains into secret vaults;
There Abendong lies, frozen at 24.
His life drowned in myths by innocent children;
His death will be their death if they dare forget.

Refrain: The children of the hearth have come

They scour the living rooms of yesterday,
flipping through albums of betrayed dreams.
Trapped flashes illuminate frozen images
of ancestors waiting for an overdue libation.

Refrain: The children of the hearth have come

A SONG IN THE SHOWER

You didn't know I was listening
As you sang in the shower.
It was a simple old song
But it jolted the strings of my past.
The arrows of water poked my heart when you asked:
"Where's your Momma gone?"*
I answered in our living room in Buea
Where Mama dusted her LP brought from London.
 You lathered soap and intoned
"Where's your Poppa gone"
I felt a sting in both eyes.
And answered by Papa's Grundig gramophone
Another memory of two lives I carry.
You did not see me wipe the tears nor hear me whisper:
"Far, far away
 Far, far away"
 You did not see me bury my head in both hands and
        rock my body.
You came out in your towel smiling
I smiled back, got up and we chorused: Chirpy, Chirpy,
        Cheep
"ooh wee chirpy chirpy cheep cheep
chirpy chirpy cheep cheep chirp"
Singing my past into my present.

* From "Chirpy Chirpy Cheep Cheep", a 1971 song by British pop
band, Middle of the Road.

A DIGITAL MOMENT

After so long, I am finally in your
Digital presence. Seeing is believing!

You unbutton my blouse with your eyelids
My nipples stare at your brown manly chest

Your passionate gaze forces my lips apart
Like a helpless fish on a sandy shore

You rise in front of my very own eyes
Standing tall and nodding in admiration

I twist and turn on the rhythm of my pulse
Doing my choreography of desire

Any moment now the screen will give way…
It's been so long in coming; oh so long!

FORGET-ME-NOT

When I was a child I measured my steps
With bright flowers on the narrow
Shortcuts to school. Two flowers I still remember:
The sunflower at the start of my journey.
It's petals like the sun lit my way
I touched it not for fear I would delay
But for every "Forget-me-not"
I stopped and picked a bunch
They were near my journey's end.
The white, blue and purple
Always seduced my youthful eyes
I rubbed them on my sweaty nose;
 brushed them softly against my lips.
Many years have gone by, but
there's something I want you to know:
Each time you rub your nose against mine
And part my lips so softly
My soul whispers tenderly…
"Forget-me-not"

IDENTITY

You tell me you did not fall from a tree.
You have a father, and you want his name.
Today you carry a piece of paper with
A new name, a flash light of identity.

They say I am a good woman
Because I do not tell how your father laughed
At the love that brought him into my thighs,
And hung my hymen like a pendant on his neck.

They say I am a real African woman
Because I do not tell of my nine-month agony:
His mother mocking my mother at the market place,
Saying his son was no fool to fall for trash like me

They say my stomach is a guarded store
Because I do not tell you that my brain
Could find x even in the absence of y,
But your father's P made me a slut fit for no school

They say I have the wisdom of a tortoise
Because I allowed your father to drive that big car
Through our family's pain
In exchange for that sought-after visa to a foreign land

They say you must be grateful to me
Because I gave up my life for yours,
But my child, a paper is a paper
Your identity is beyond paper! Someday!

Eric Ngalle Charles

Iya

Loud is the chorus
On the highlands of 'Weli'

Loud barking noise
As 'Mokoti Mo Ngwa'
Chases the Njuwe.
the forest swayed,
left and then right

Loud again the chorus
On the highlands of 'Weli'

Today as Iya Efeti smiles
Happiness takes refuge in my heart.

Libations by my ancestors
remove the garments of an outcast.

Wana wa Nyuwe "the orphaned children"

In my memory as a boy
I saw my mother's wrinkles

First,
when the sun came
Then,
when the rains came
again,
when dust came.
Then,
nothing came.

Her daughters were hungry.

My mother grovelled from dawn to dusk for a glass of milk,
slaved for bottled iodine
A cure for berry berry, maybe Kwashiorkor, I thought.

As a boy,
I loved the soil,

I planted yams
I planted coco yams
plantains I planted,
Beans, potatoes, my earthly friends .

When my uncle took a second wife
I gave her tadpoles,

My uncle laughed,
When the doors closed
they consumed palm wine.
they laughed

"The bastard child sold his fatherland" they said

before meals we prayed
After meals we prayed
Our God is blind, They said
My mother said "today the harvest is poor"

She went and married 'Ndondondume' he crowed, he quacked, an impostor

I saw how my mothers bones
they strangled her face.

First the goat
Then the pig
Then two chickens

In my memory as a boy
My many fathers emptied my mother's Kraal.

One by one they left

I wished they do not return,
They didn't.

And place my shadow gently
into a cupboard.

watch as she sleeps,
this night be her last
between two beasts
and the bottomless pit.

she descends, she whispers,
her tongue behind her lips.

Tonight the moon is sinful
her breathing fast
her dreams barefooted.

Nothing hostile about her smiles?

You wish.

As the sun departs,
I will write a love poem in your palm.

On the bark of a green leaf,
I shall paint in yellow ink.

As the world blinks,
as shadows roam,
I will plead with passing birds,
to carry me to you.

I will shout to the mountains,

'I love you'

The mountains retort,

'Your lover is dead'

Iya: mother of many children.

L - #0132 - 290120 - C0 - 210/148/13 - PB - DID2753401